ABC
Date Nights

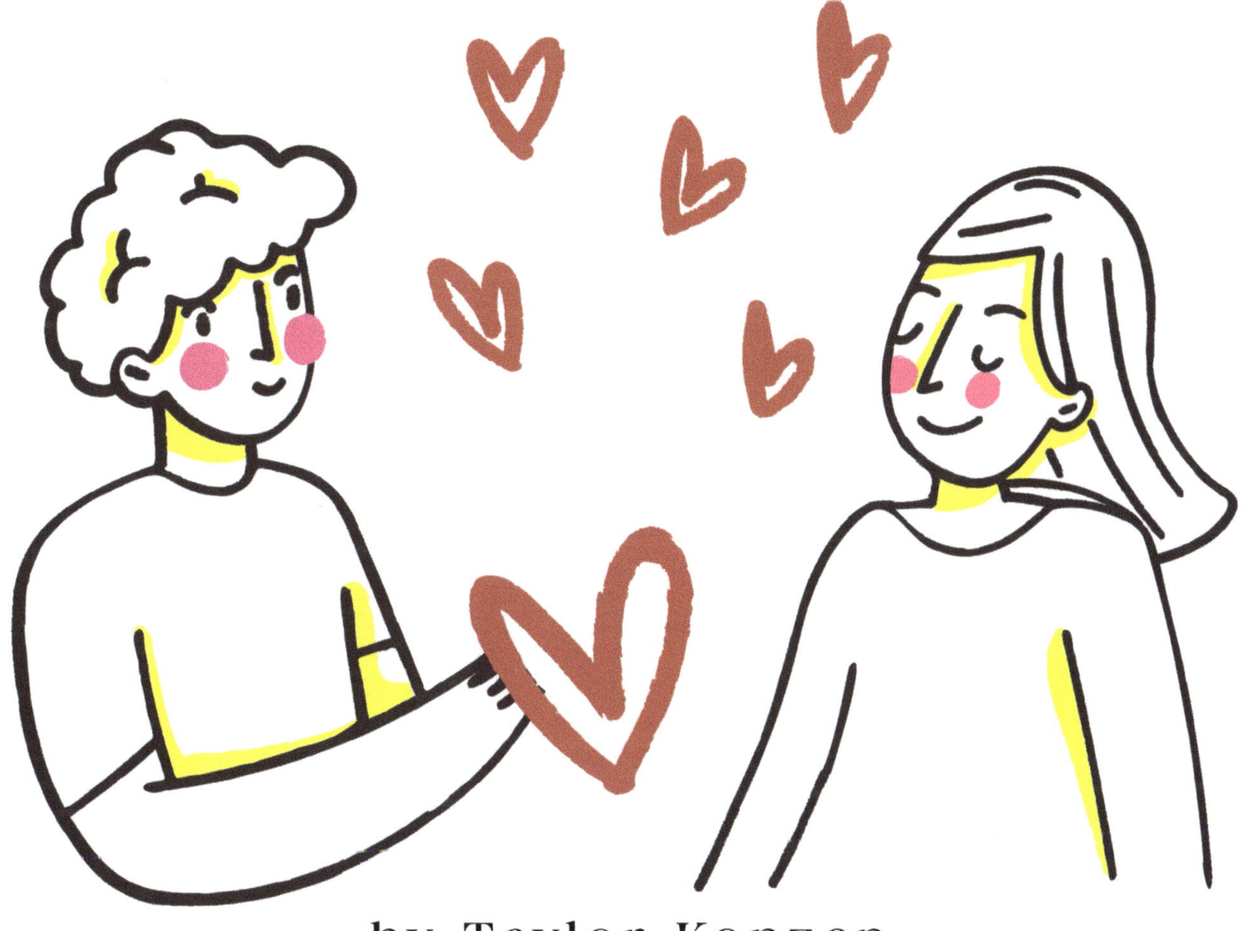

by Taylor Konzen

Date nights based around the alphabet are the best way to creatively come up with a simple date.

It is sometimes hard to come up with new ideas for dates, alphabet date ideas can help you overcome those difficullies.We have over 1,000 date ideas based on the alphabet.

Be sure to take a picture as your completing the date, and paste it onto the polaroid mock. Don't forget to include some interesting facts about the date!

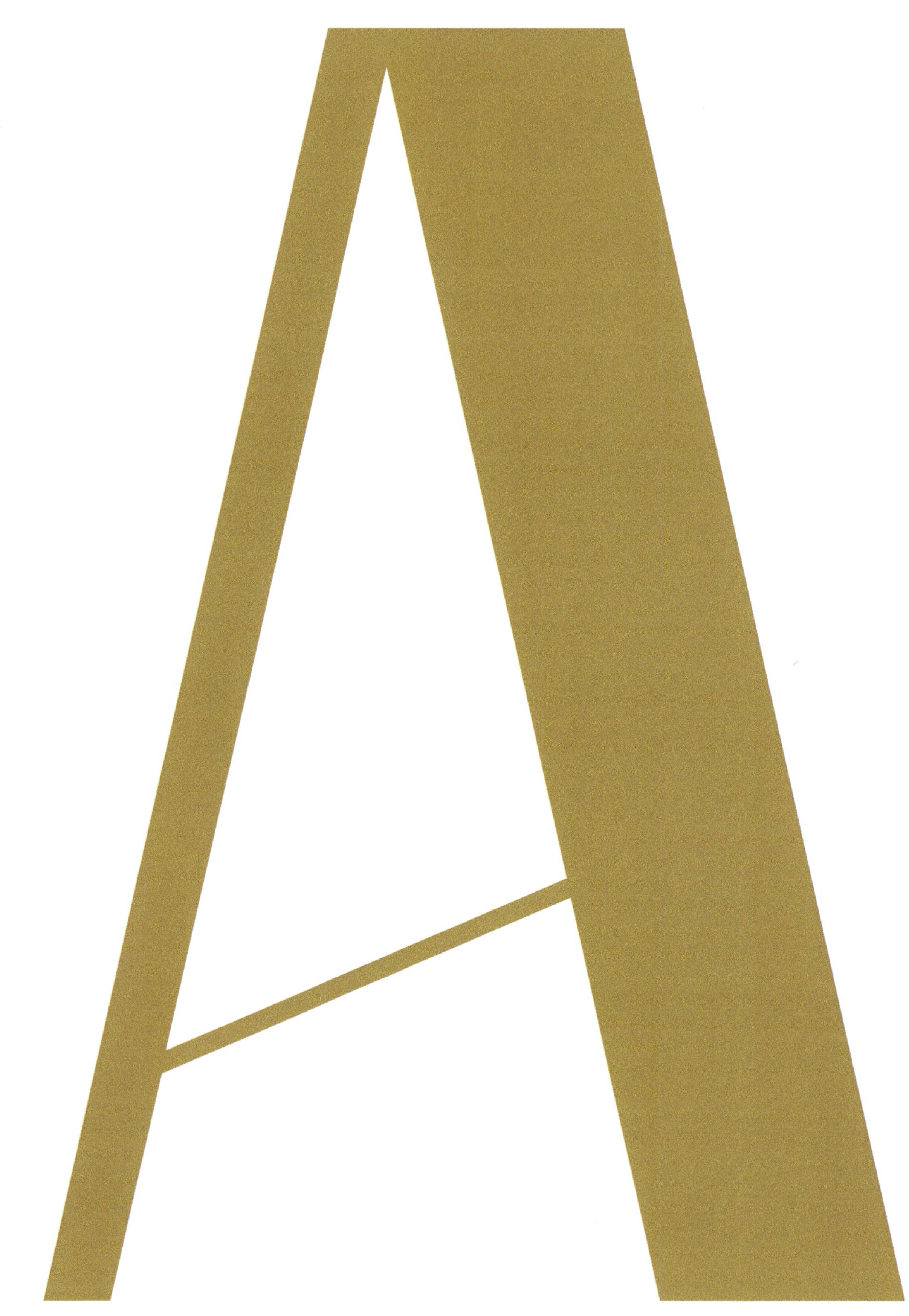

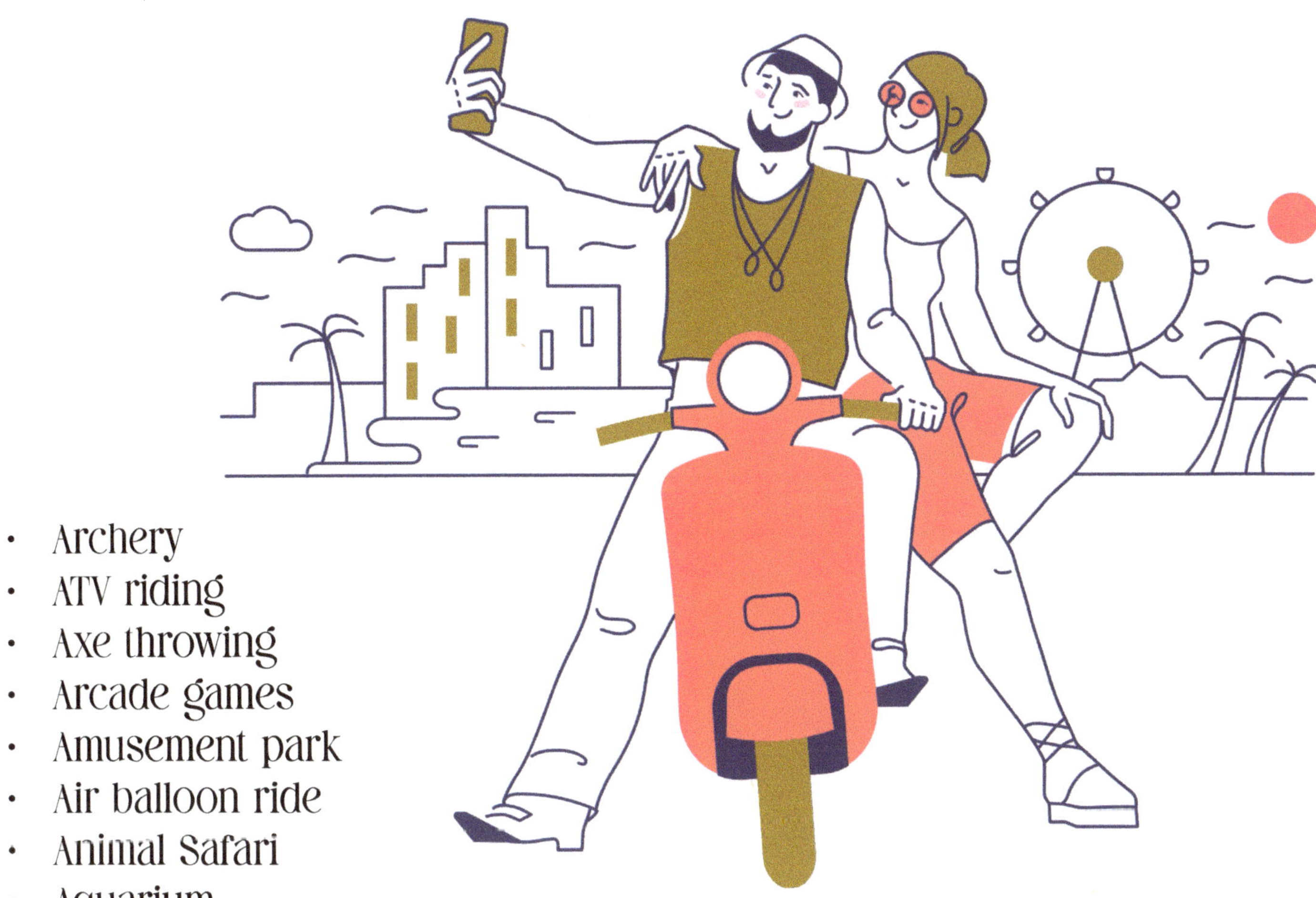

- Archery
- ATV riding
- Axe throwing
- Arcade games
- Amusement park
- Air balloon ride
- Animal Safari
- Aquarium
- Acrobatics class
- Astronomy walk
- Adventure movie marathon
- Antique store hunt
- Art museum
- Apple picking/baking
- Apple cider testing
- Alcoholic beverage making class
- At-home food tasting competition
- Art gallery
- Art festival
- Artisan jewelry making workshop
- American history museum visit
- Aqua cycling
- Astronomical Observatory visit
- Afternoon hike date until sunset
- Agility training class
- Athletic footwear shopping
- Acupuncture couples treatment
- Adult coloring book competition
- Anti-gravity class
- At-home spa day
- Animal sanctuary visit
- Animal farm visit
- Animal watching
- Airbnb stay
- Adventure road trip
- Acrylic painting class
- Acoustic guitar lesson

4 In (Height) X 6 In (Width)

Date:

____
____
____
____
____
____

2.6 In (Height)
X
2.6 In (Width)

Date:

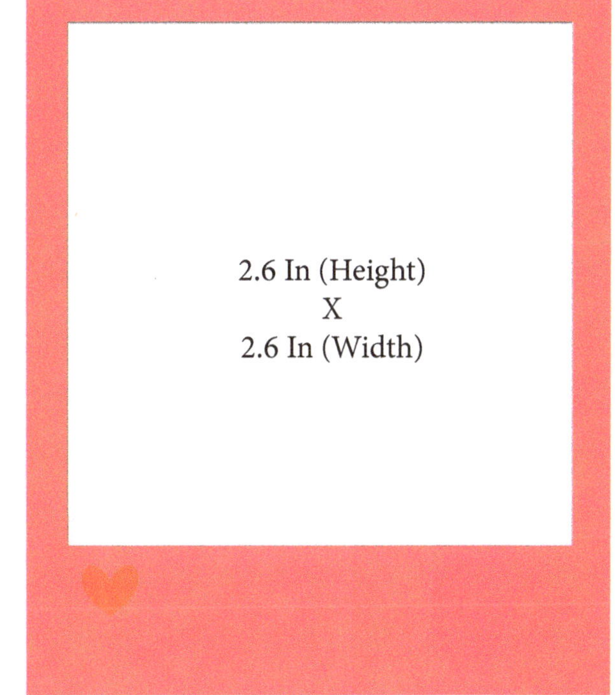

Date:

2.6 In (Height)
X
2.6 In (Width)

2.6 In (Height)
X
2.6 In (Width)

Date:

Date:

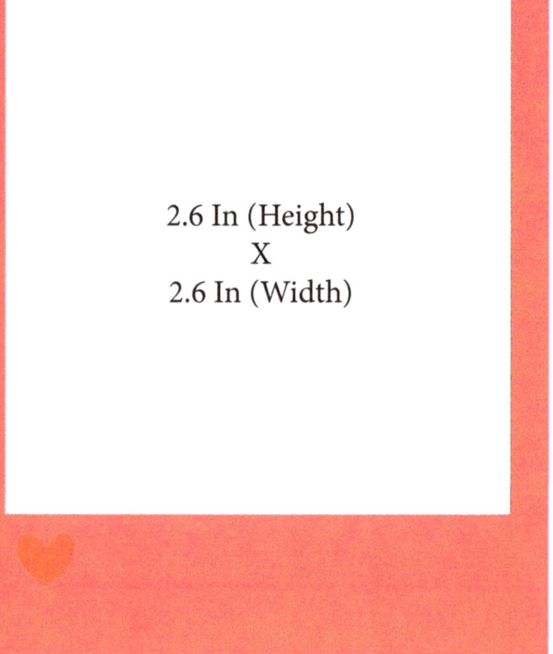

2.6 In (Height)
X
2.6 In (Width)

4 In (Height) X 6 In (Width)

Date:

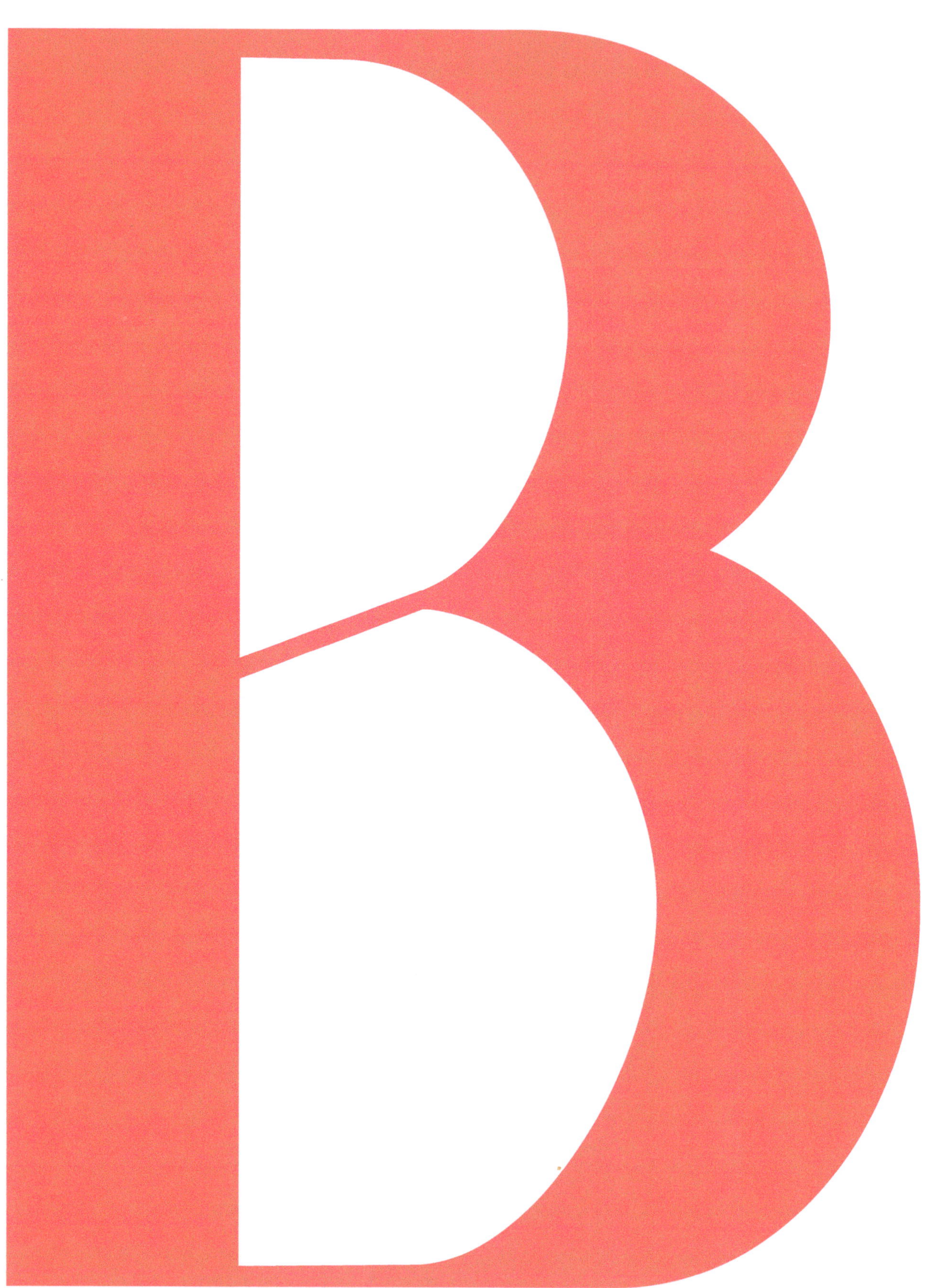

- Baby photo exchange
- Back massage exchange
- Backpacking trip
- Backrubs
- Backyard Barbecue
- Backyard firepit night
- Badminton
- Ball dance lesson
- Ballet show
- Balloon ride
- Bar hopping
- Basketball game
- Batting cage
- Beach barbecue
- Beach day
- Beach volleyball
- Bed day
- Beer & cheese tasting
- Beerfest
- Berry picking
- Bike ride
- Biking trail adventure
- Bird spotting
- Black and white movie night
- Blindfold dinner
- Board game night
- Boat cruise ride
- Boat sunset cruise
- Boating
- Body massage exchange

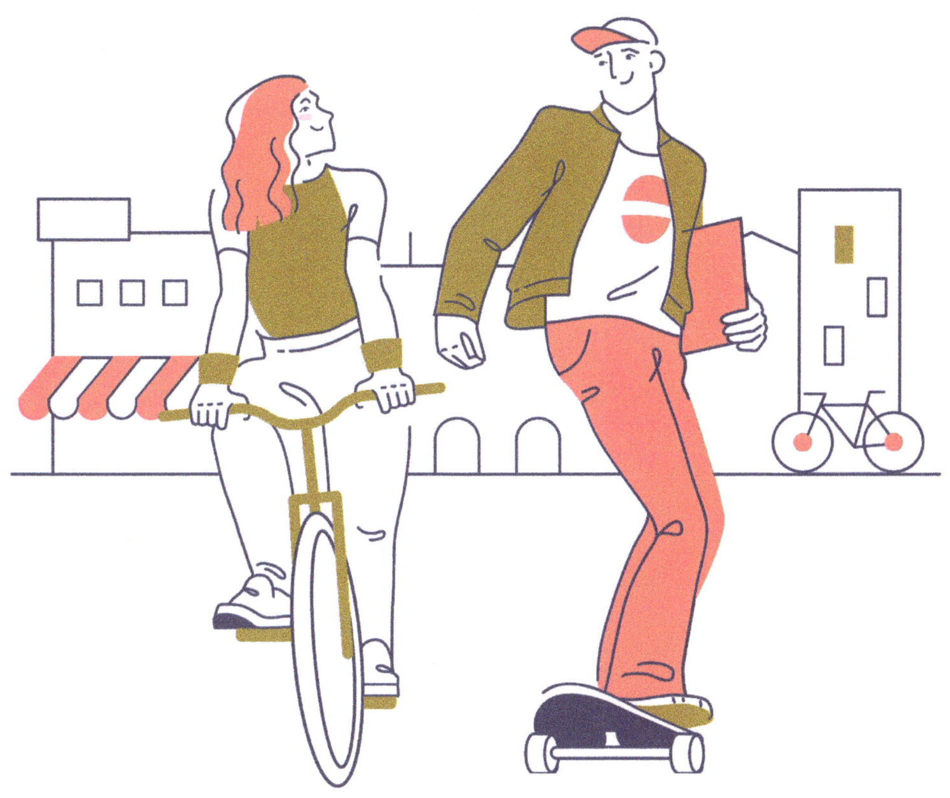

- Body painting
- Botanical garden visit
- Bowling
- Boxing game
- Breakfast in bed
- Brewery tour
- Brownie making class
- Brunch hoping
- Brunch in bed
- Brunch on a boat
- Brunch on a rooftop
- Brunch picnic
- Bubble bath
- Bubble tea date
- Build a ring together
- Bull riding at a bar
- Bungee jumping
- Butterfly conservatory visit

4 In (Height) X 6 In (Width)

Date:

____

____

____

____

____

____

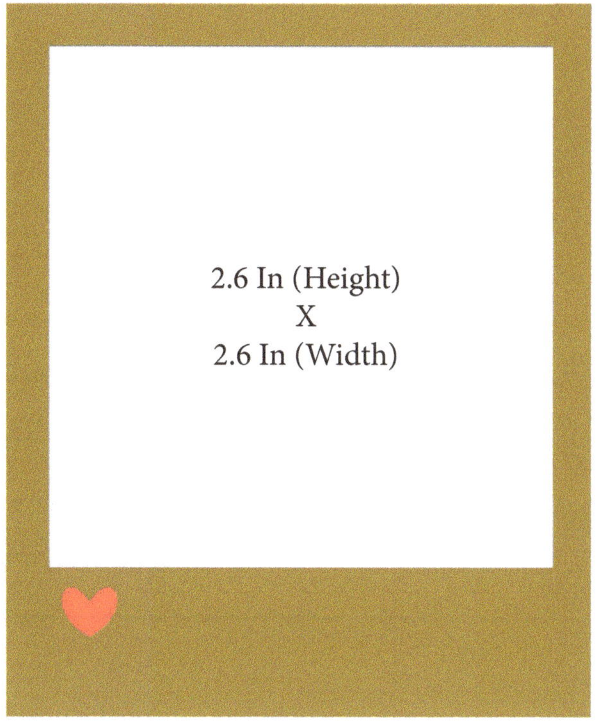

Date:

____

____

____

____

____

____

Date:

____

____

____

____

____

____

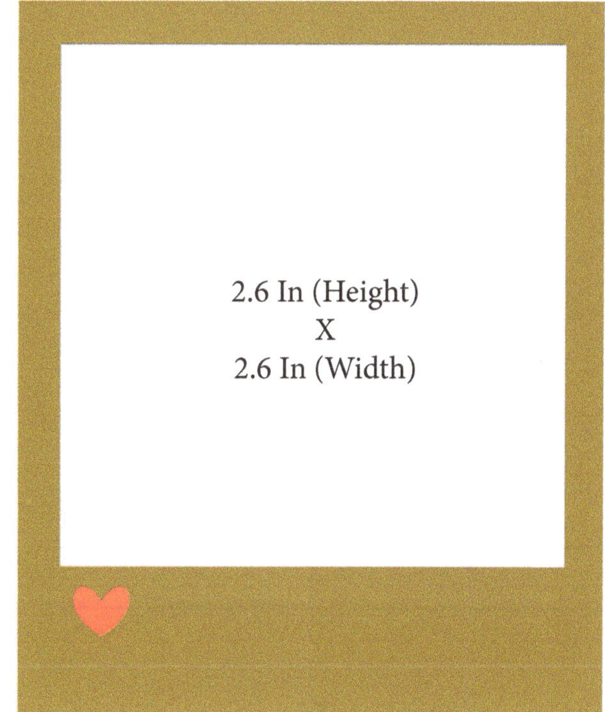

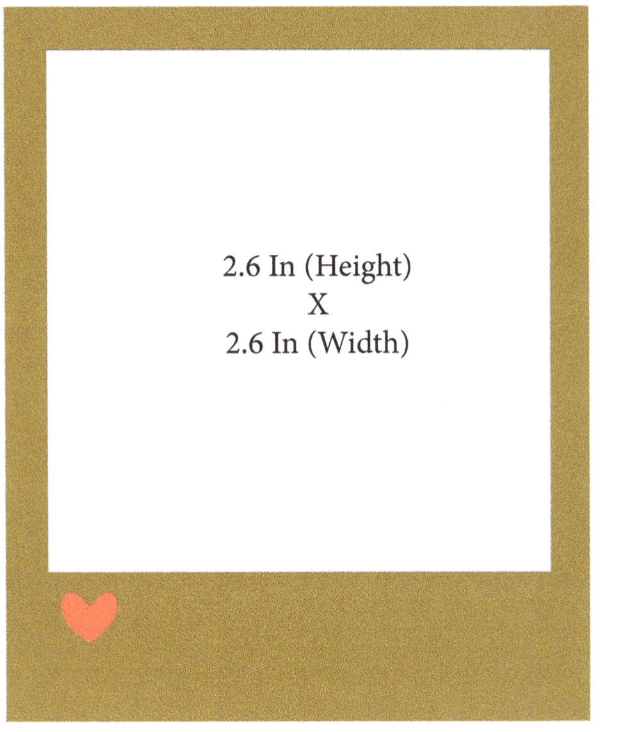

Date:

____
____
____
____
____
____

Date:

____
____
____
____
____
____

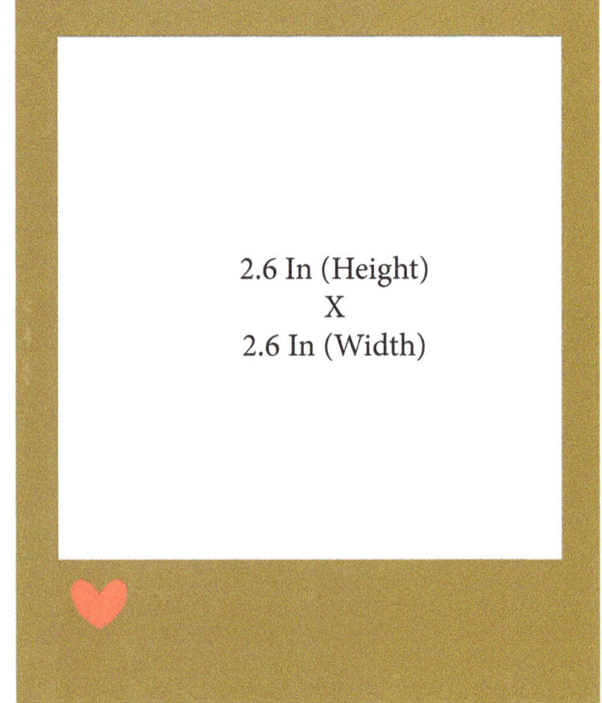

4 In (Height) X 6 In (Width)

Date:

____
____
____
____
____
____

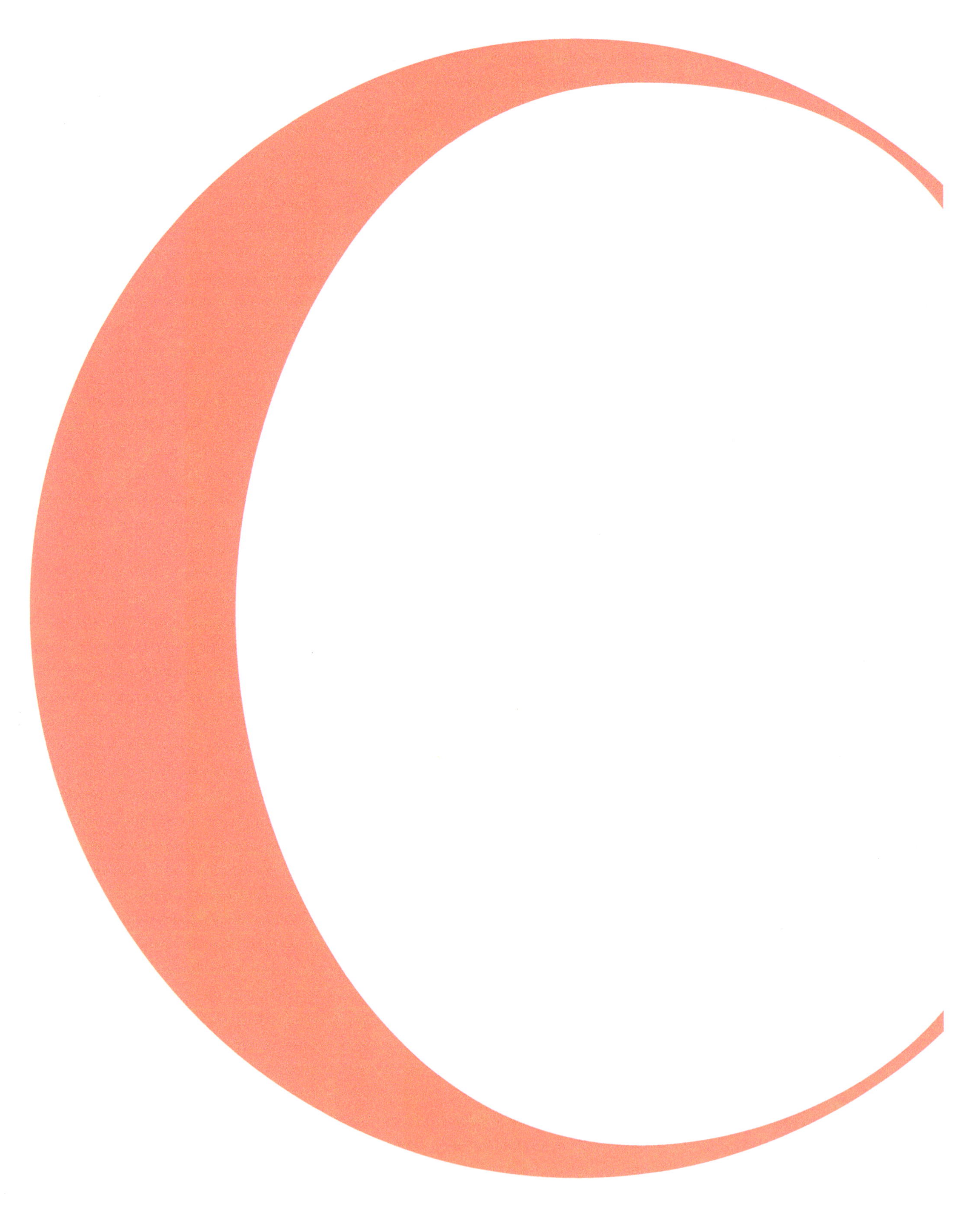

- Cake baking class
- Camping trip
- Camping under the stars
- Candle making class
- Candlelight dinner
- Candy factory
- Candy shop
- Canoeing
- Canva painting class
- Champagne breakfast
- Casino date
- Cate café date
- Cave diving
- Cave tour
- Carnival
- Cruise
- Cycling
- Cherry blossom adventure
- Cherry picking
- Cinema outside
- Circus visit
- Cloud watching
- Clubbing
- Cocktail bar crawl
- Cocktail making competition
- Coffee shop date
- College sporting event
- Color run
- Color-themed picnic
- Coloring date
- Comedy club show
- Concert
- Cooking-classes
- Cooking competition
- Cornmage
- Cornhole competition
- County fair
- Couple massages
- CrossFit class
- Restaurants that start with a C

4 In (Height) X 6 In (Width)

Date:

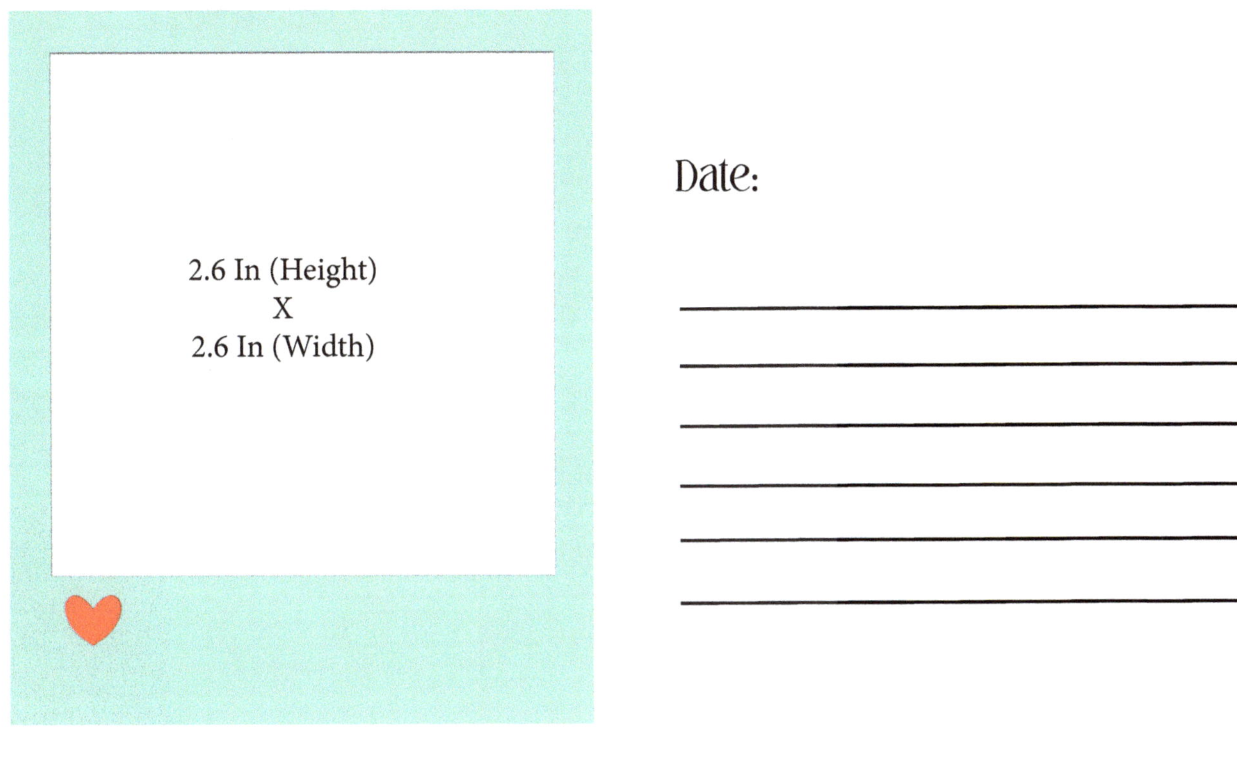

Date:

Date:

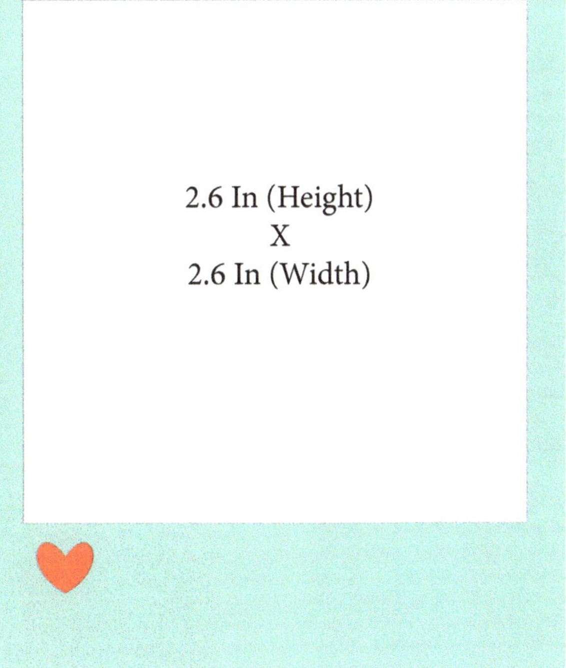

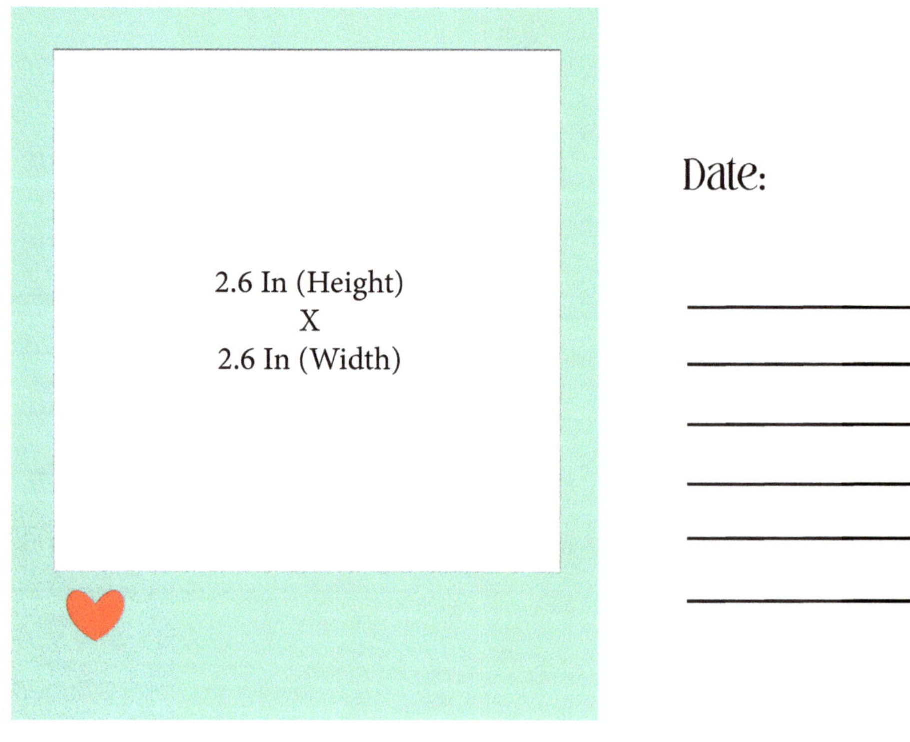

Date:

____

____

____

____

____

____

Date:

____

____

____

____

____

____

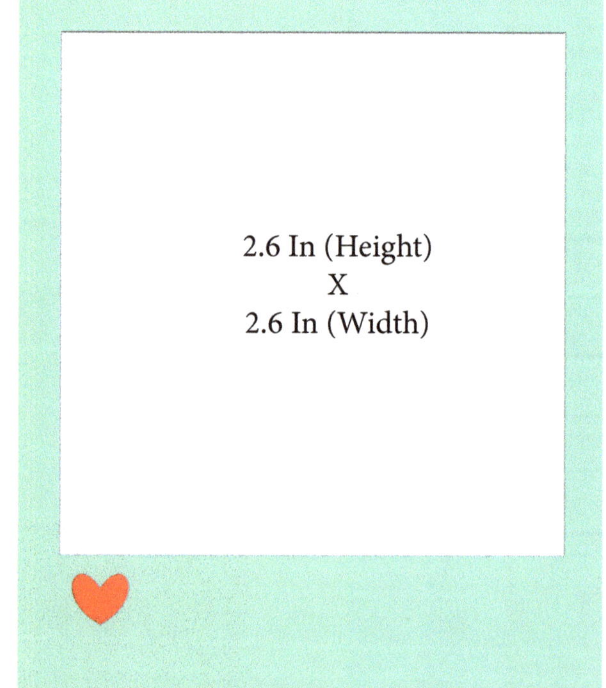

4 In (Height) X 6 In (Width)

Date:

____
____
____
____
____
____

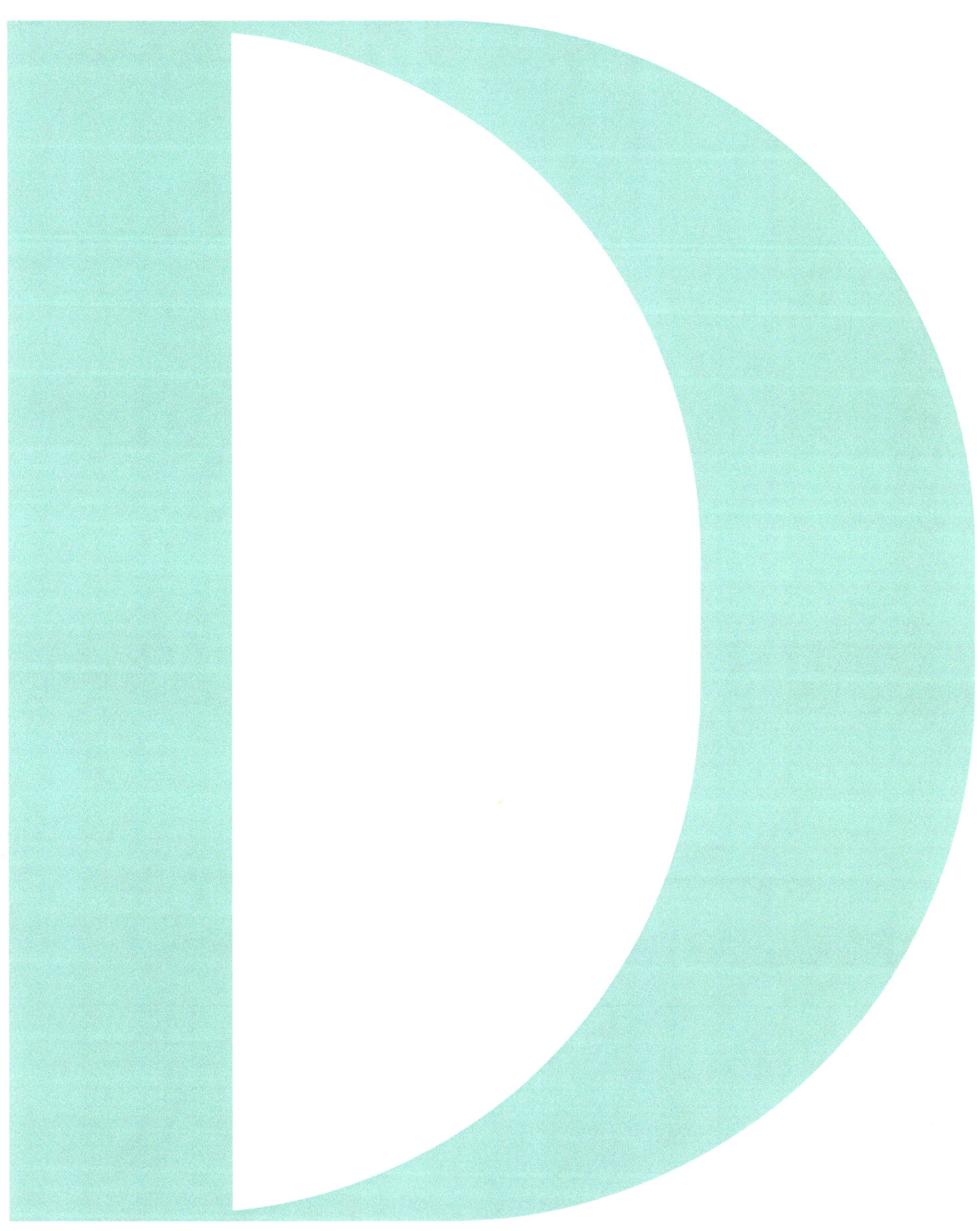

- Dairy Queen run
- Dance class
- Downtown exploration
- Darts date
- Dave & Busters
- Day trip
- Dessert sampling
- Dinner at a restaurant
- Dinner at home
- Disney Movie
- Disney trip
- Distillery tour
- Diving competition
- DIY at-home spa day
- Dodgeball
- Dog walk on the beach
- Dog walking hike
- Double date
- Doughnut shop
- Dancing
- Drive-in movie
- Driving range
- Duck feeding
- Dumplings on the beach
- Daisy picking
- Dahlia picking
- Design custom jewelry
- Decorate for the next upcoming holiday with holiday music playing
- Dollar tree gift exchange
- Donate clothes together
- Dolphin watching
- Destination date
- Demo a house together
- Deep tissue couple's massage
- Dirt bike riding
- Deer/duck hunting
- Dog park

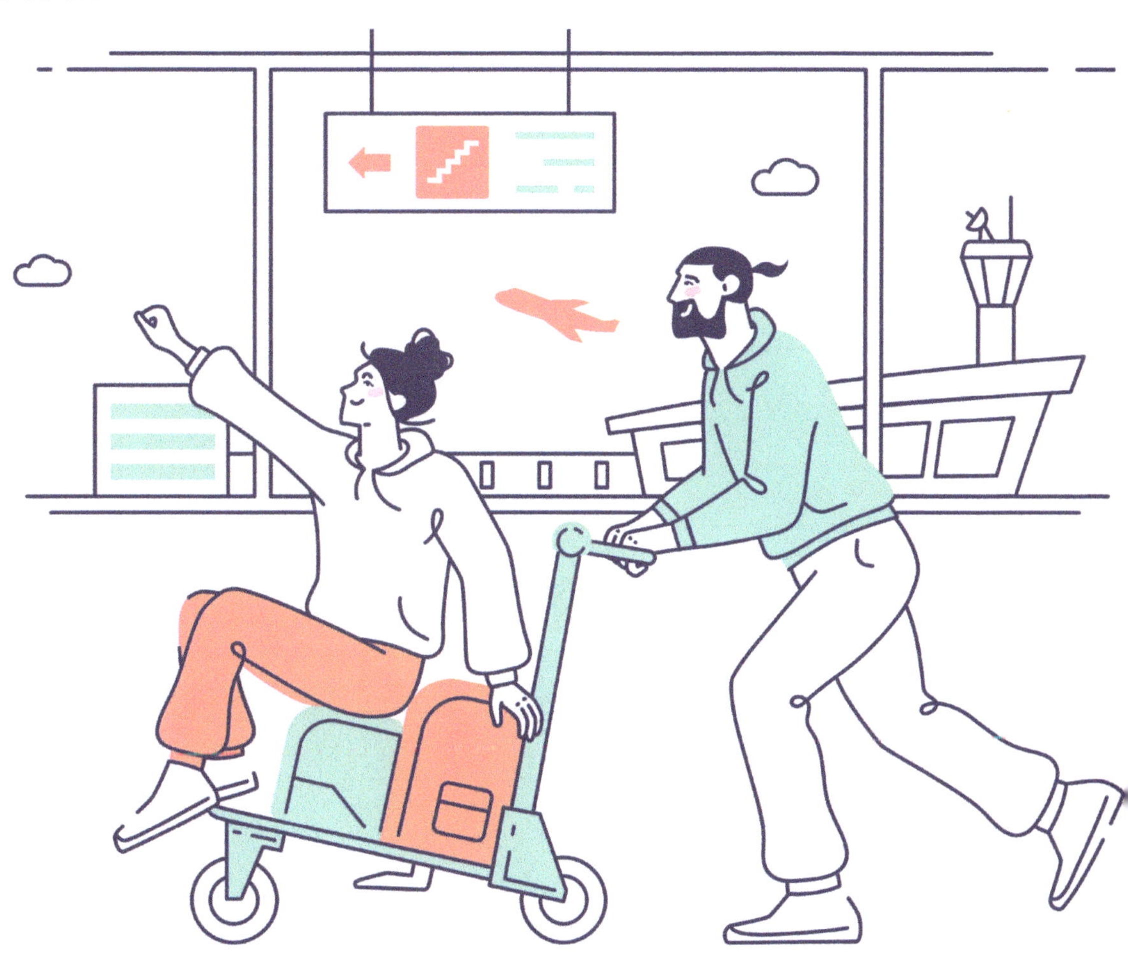

4 In (Height) X 6 In (Width)

Date:

____

____

____

____

____

____

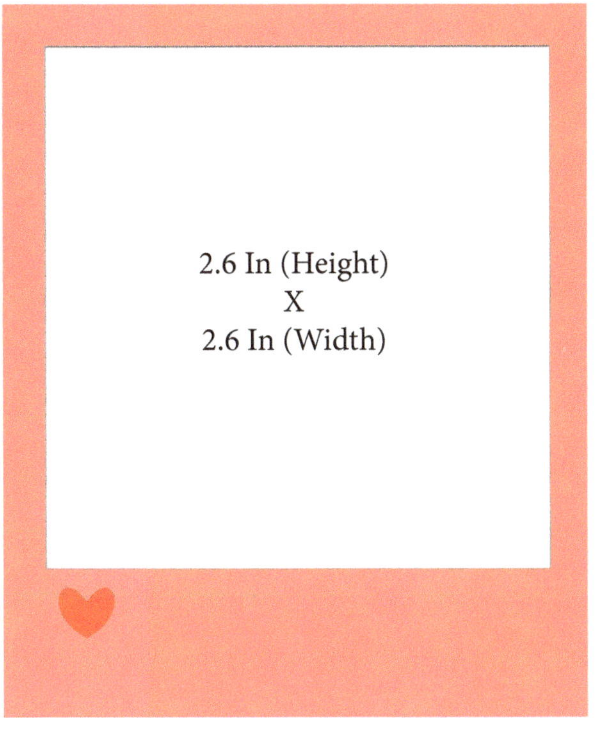

Date:

____

____

____

____

____

____

Date:

____

____

____

____

____

____

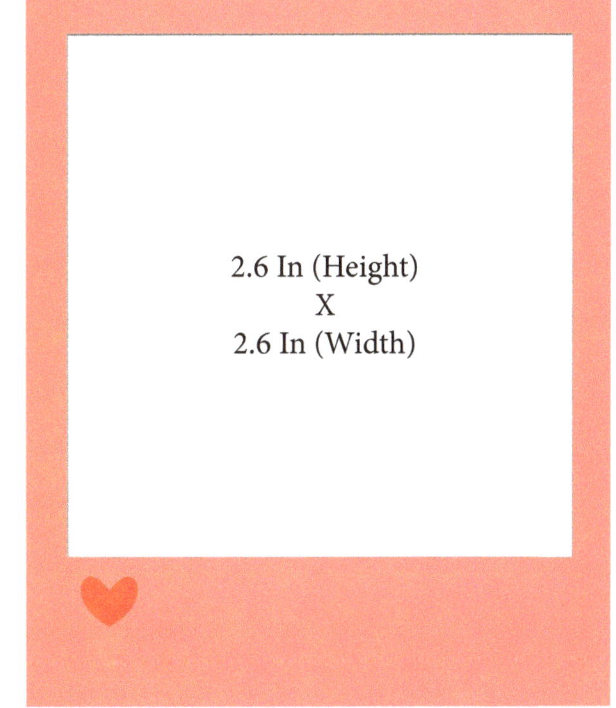

2.6 In (Height)
X
2.6 In (Width)

Date:

Date:

2.6 In (Height)
X
2.6 In (Width)

4 In (Height) X 6 In (Width)

Date:
____
____
____
____
____
____

- Escape room
- Exotic vacation
- Exhibit date
- Exercise together
- Extreme sports
- Exchange massages
- Easter egg coloring
- Early bird date
- Expensive date night
- Egyptian themed date
- Explore something new
- Eggnog tasting
- Espresso tasting
- ESPN game night
- Evening stroll
- Explore a new city
- Escape to a resort
- Engagement party ideas
- Equestrian show
- Elope
- Eiffel tower

4 In (Height) X 6 In (Width)

Date:
____
____
____
____
____
____

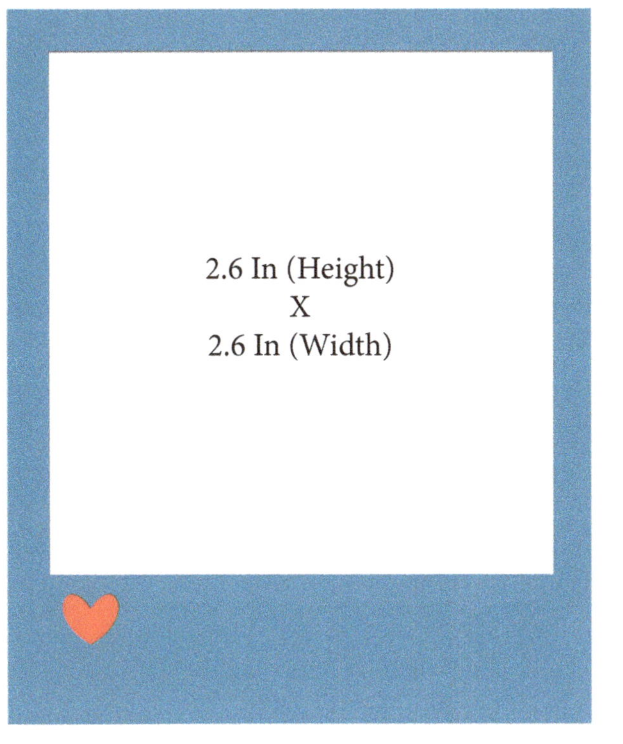

Date:

____

____

____

____

____

____

Date:

____

____

____

____

____

____

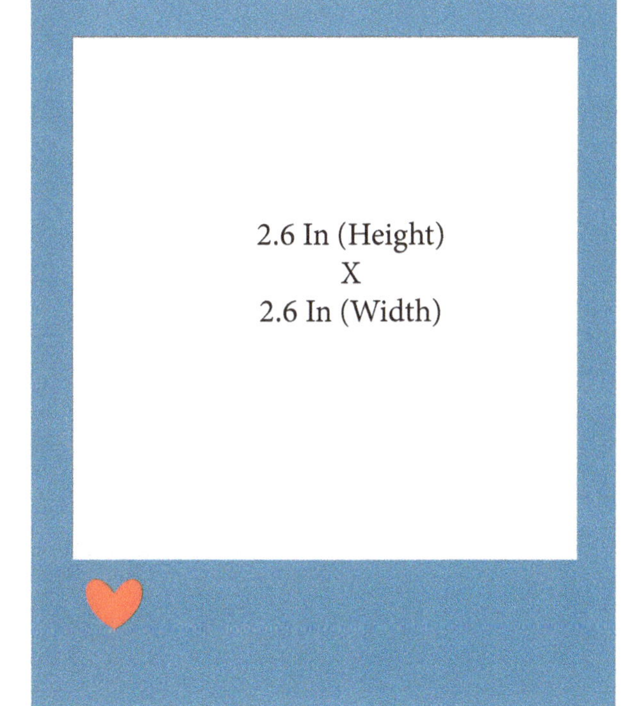

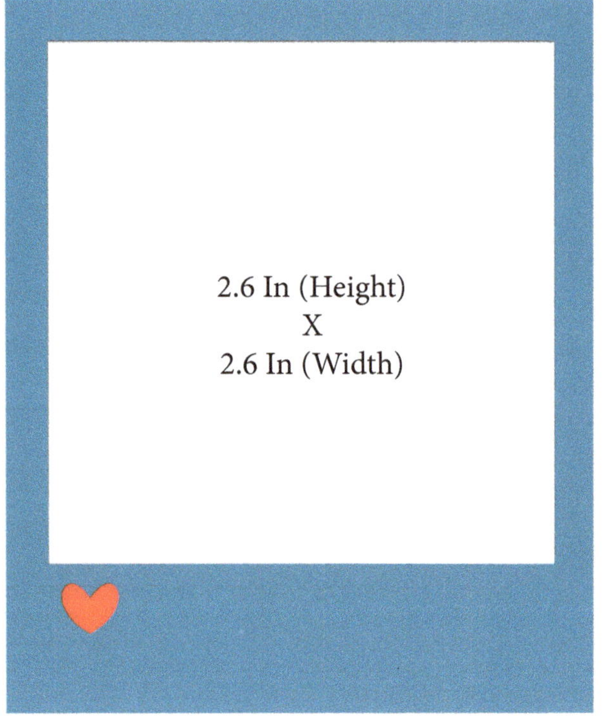

Date:

____

____

____

____

____

____

Date:

____

____

____

____

____

____

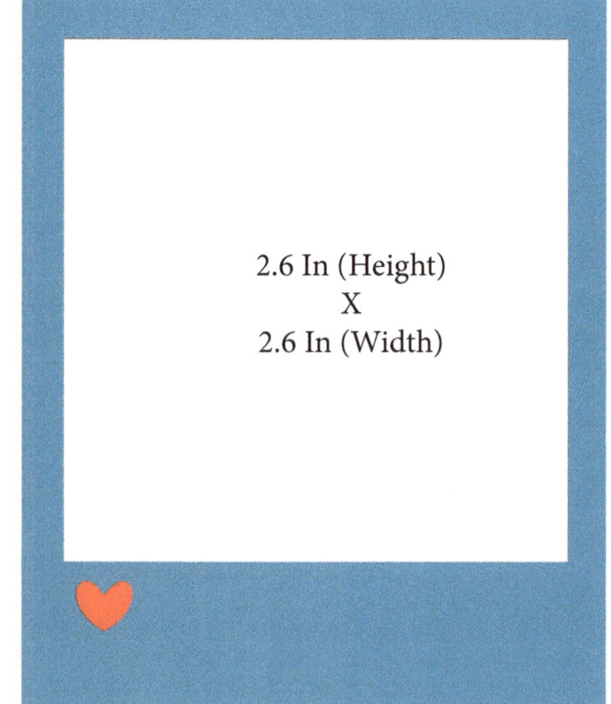

4 In (Height) X 6 In (Width)

Date:

____

____

____

____

____

____

- Flower arranging
- Food tour
- Fondue making
- Fishing
- Festival
- Fair
- Ferris wheel
- Fire (bonfire)
- Firework show
- Farmer's market visit
- Food date
- Fruit picking
- Finger foods only
- Farm adventure
- Factory tour
- Flea market
- Four wheeling
- Foot massage exchange
- Full body exchange
- Facial exchange
- Fancy restaurant date
- Fitness class
- Frisbee catch
- Football game
- Foosball competition
- Final four Basketball game
- Fight night
- Fashion show
- Face painting class
- Foam Dance party
- Film festival
- Fajita making
- Fortune cookie readings

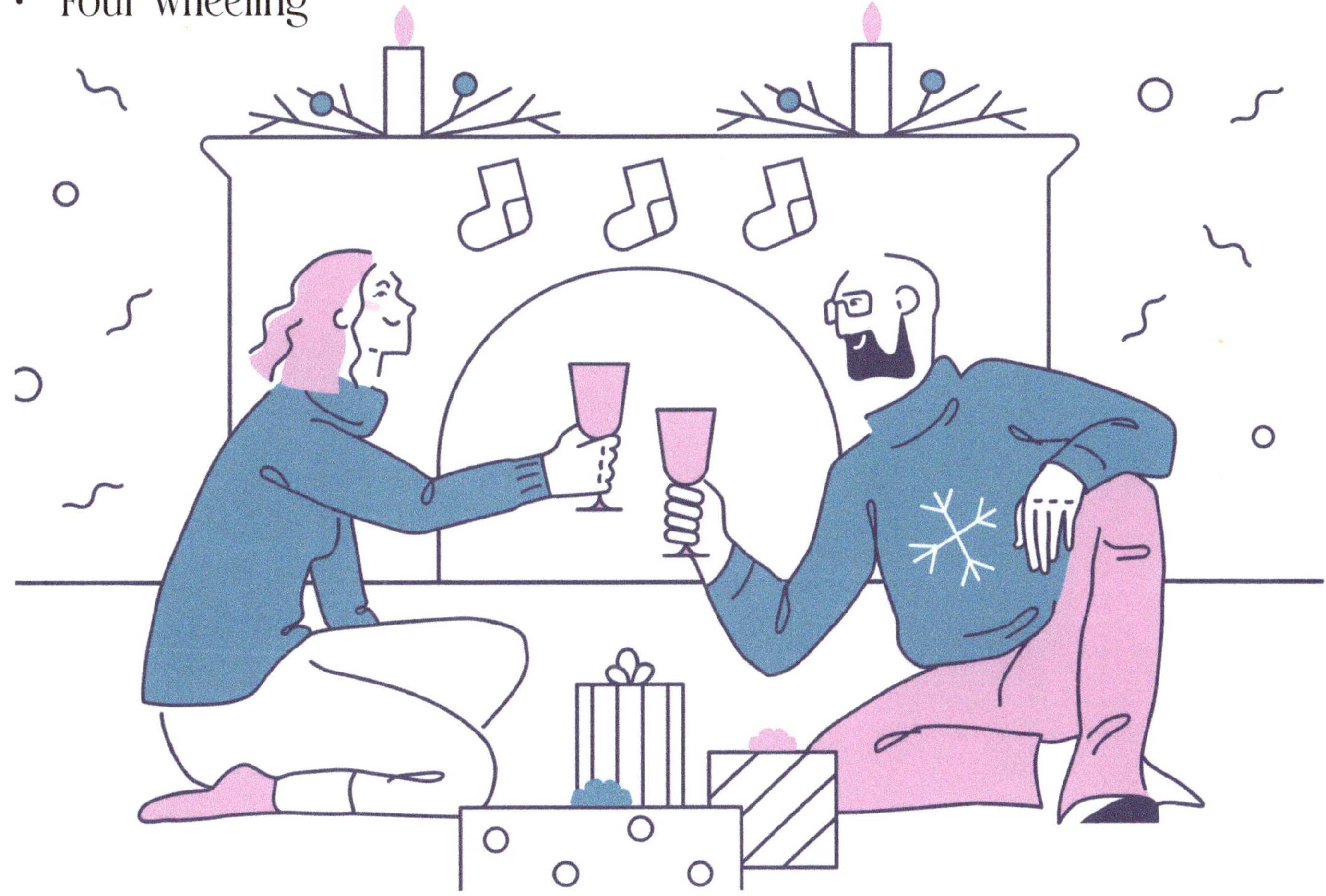

4 In (Height) X 6 In (Width)

Date:

____

____

____

____

____

____

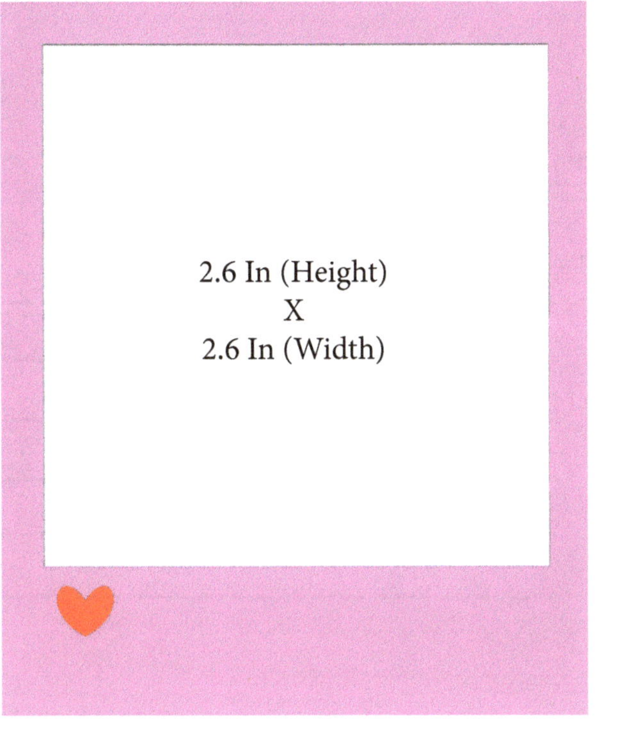

Date:

____

____

____

____

____

____

Date:

____

____

____

____

____

____

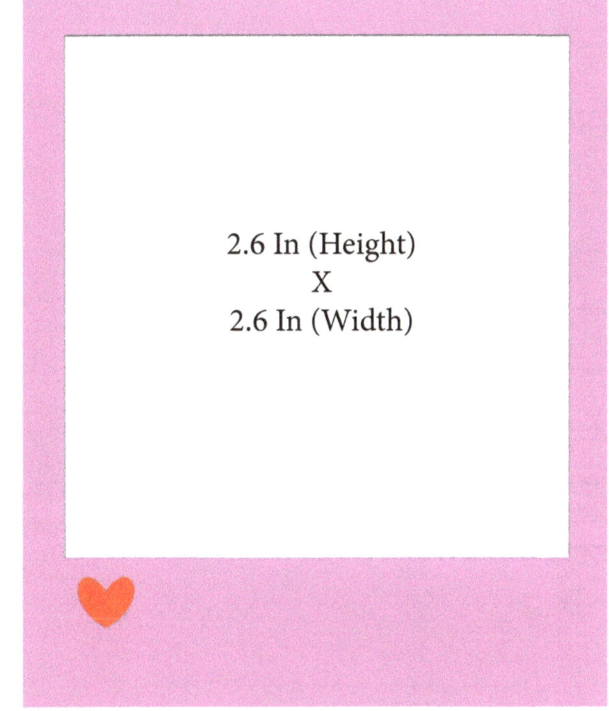

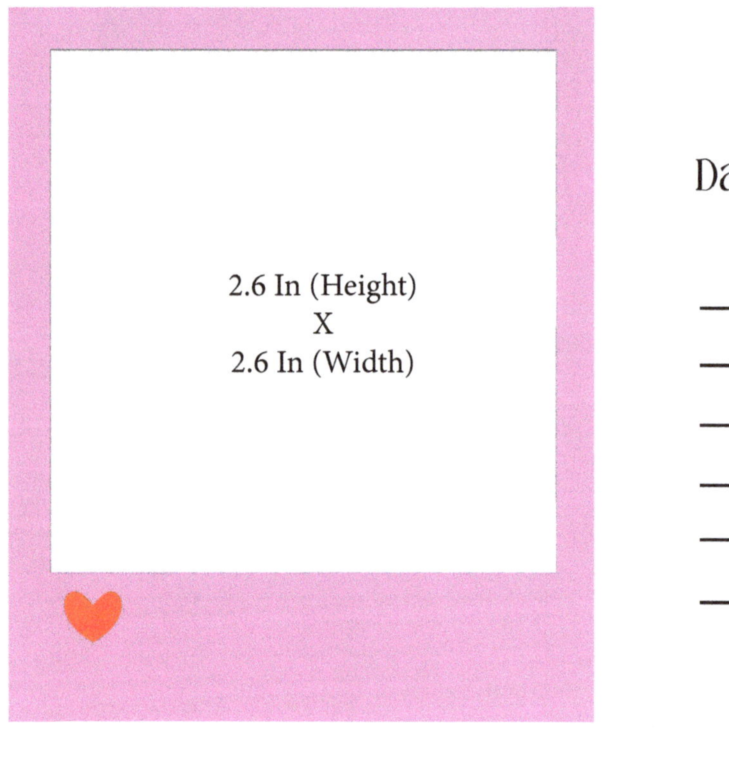

Date:

____

____

____

____

____

____

Date:

____

____

____

____

____

____

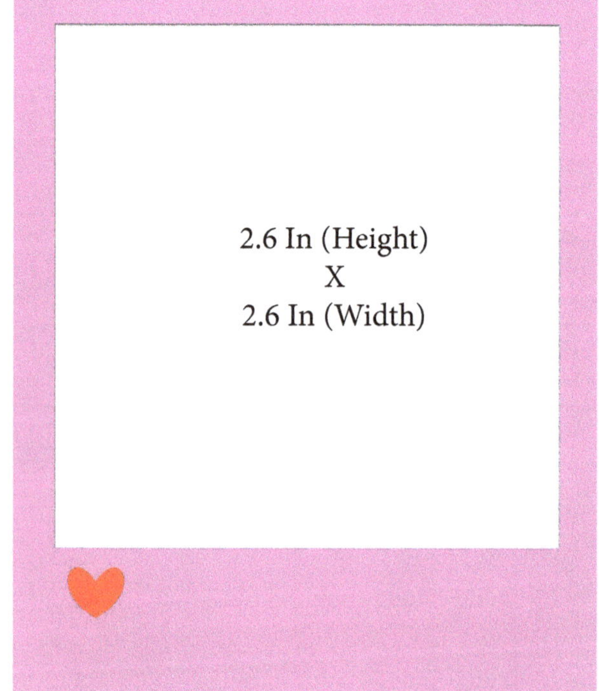

4 In (Height) X 6 In (Width)

Date:

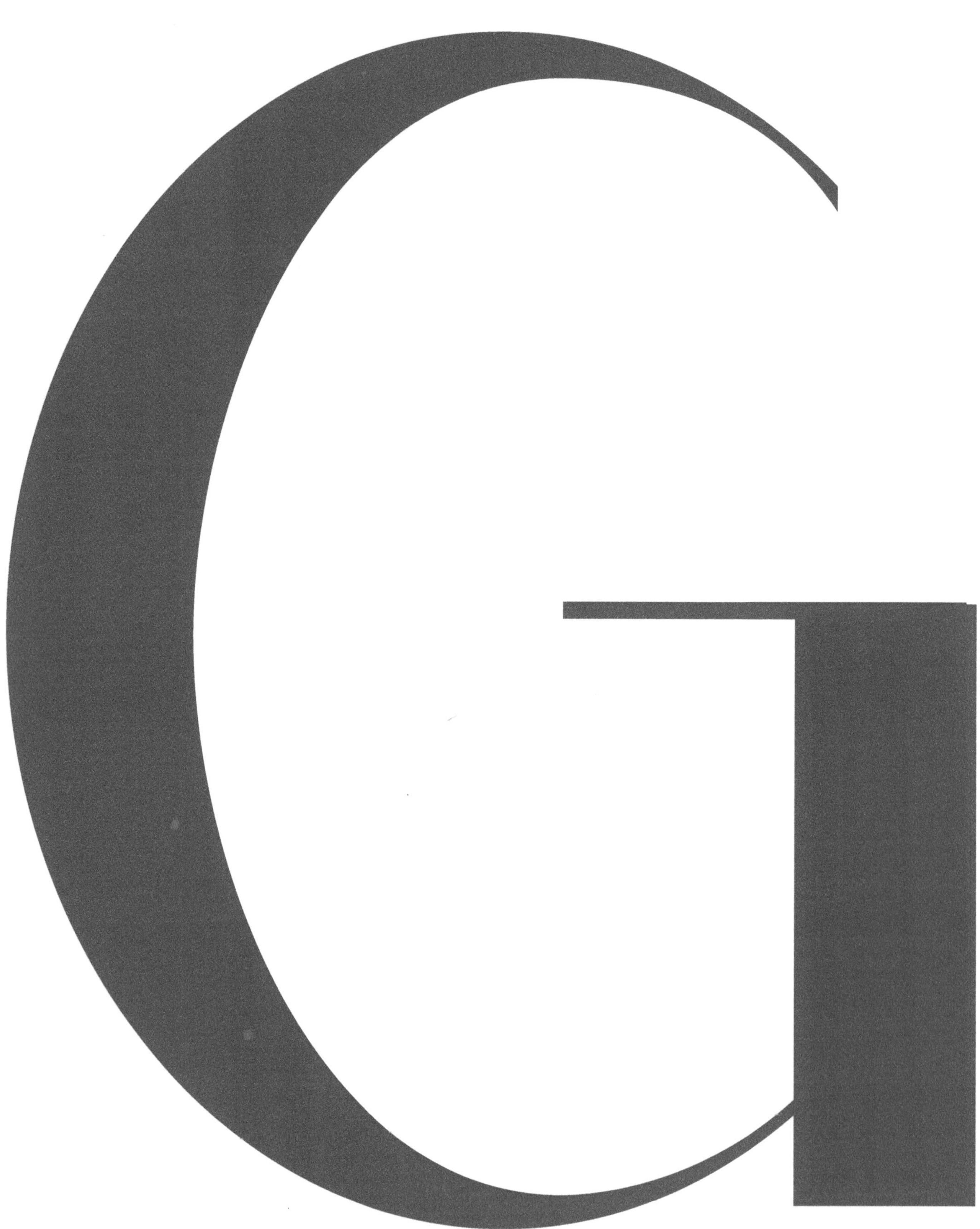

- Game night
- Glassblowing class
- Golf
- Go-karts
- Gun range
- Gambling
- Gardening
- Grocery store date
- Grilling master date
- Gourmet cooking class
- Ghost tour
- Guitar lessons
- Gymnastics meet
- Go-pro adventure
- Gingerbread house contest
- Go somewhere new
- Guacamole making
- Gourmet dining
- Gelato date

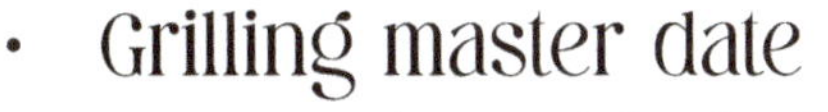
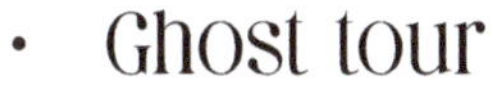

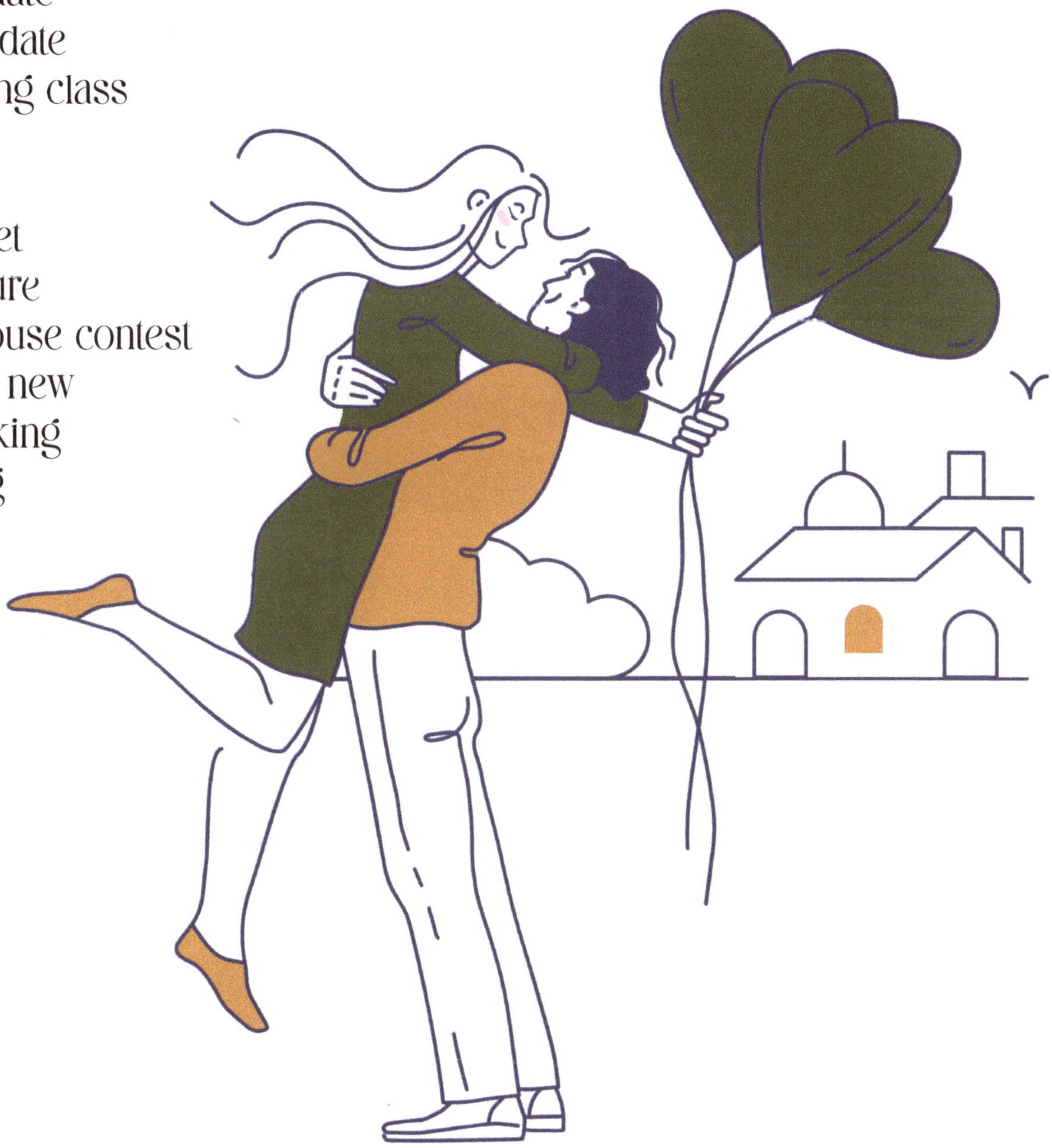

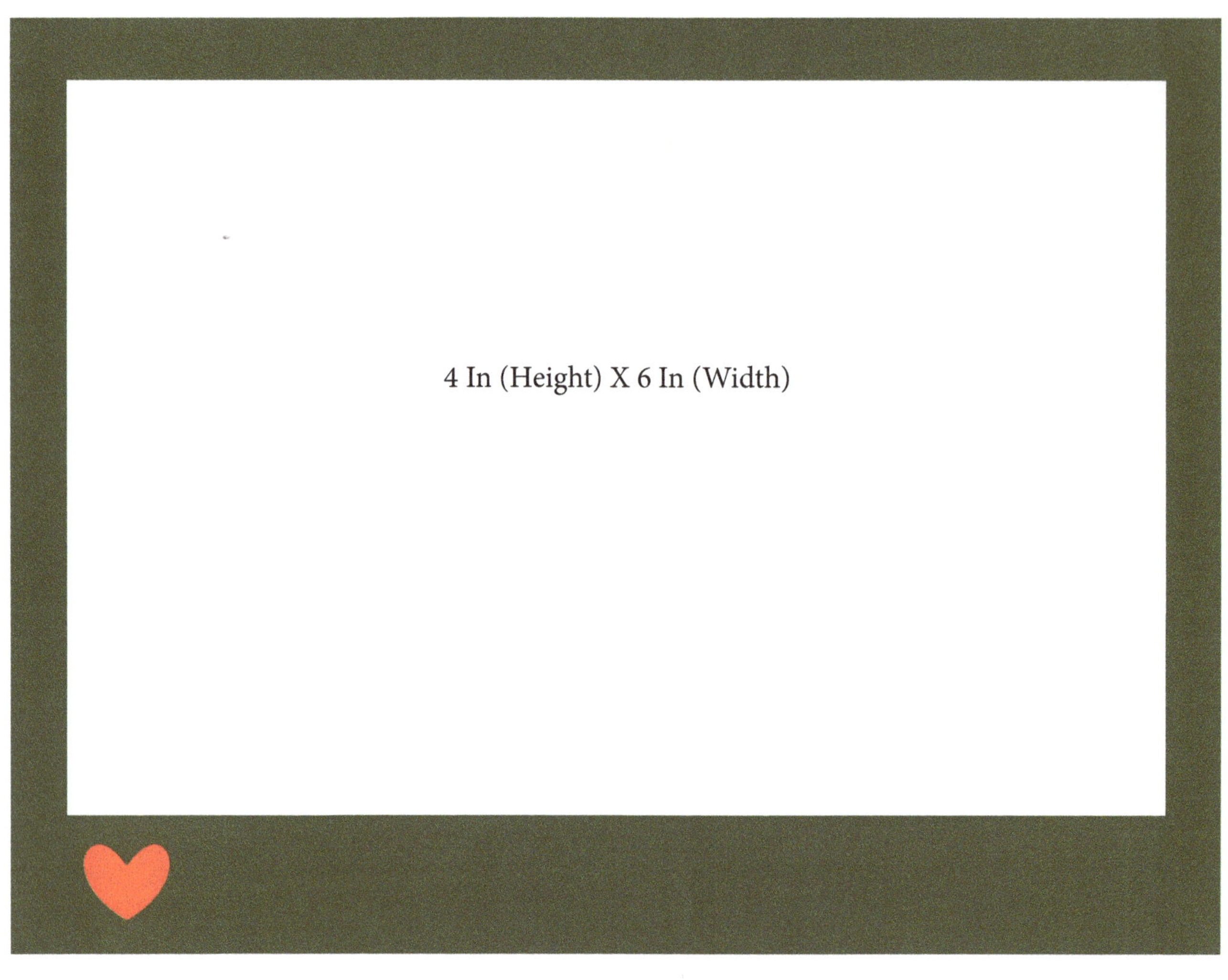

Date:

____
____
____
____
____
____

2.6 In (Height)
X
2.6 In (Width)

Date:

Date:

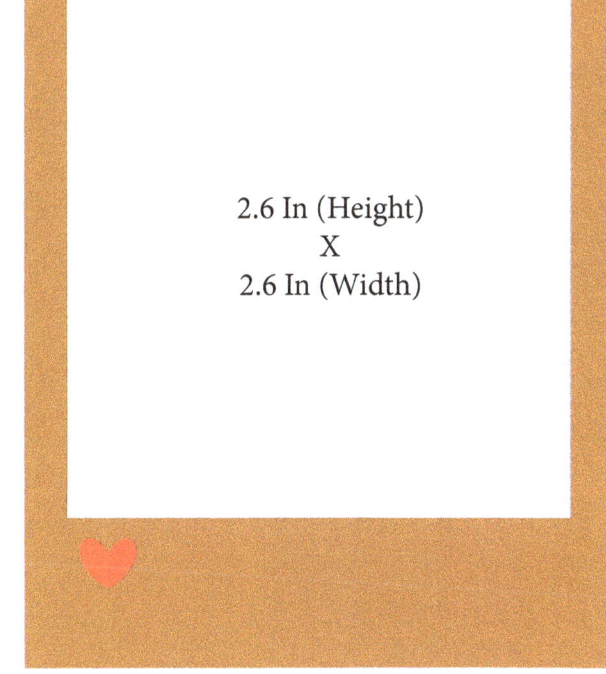

2.6 In (Height)
X
2.6 In (Width)

2.6 In (Height)
X
2.6 In (Width)

2.6 In (Height)
X
2.6 In (Width)

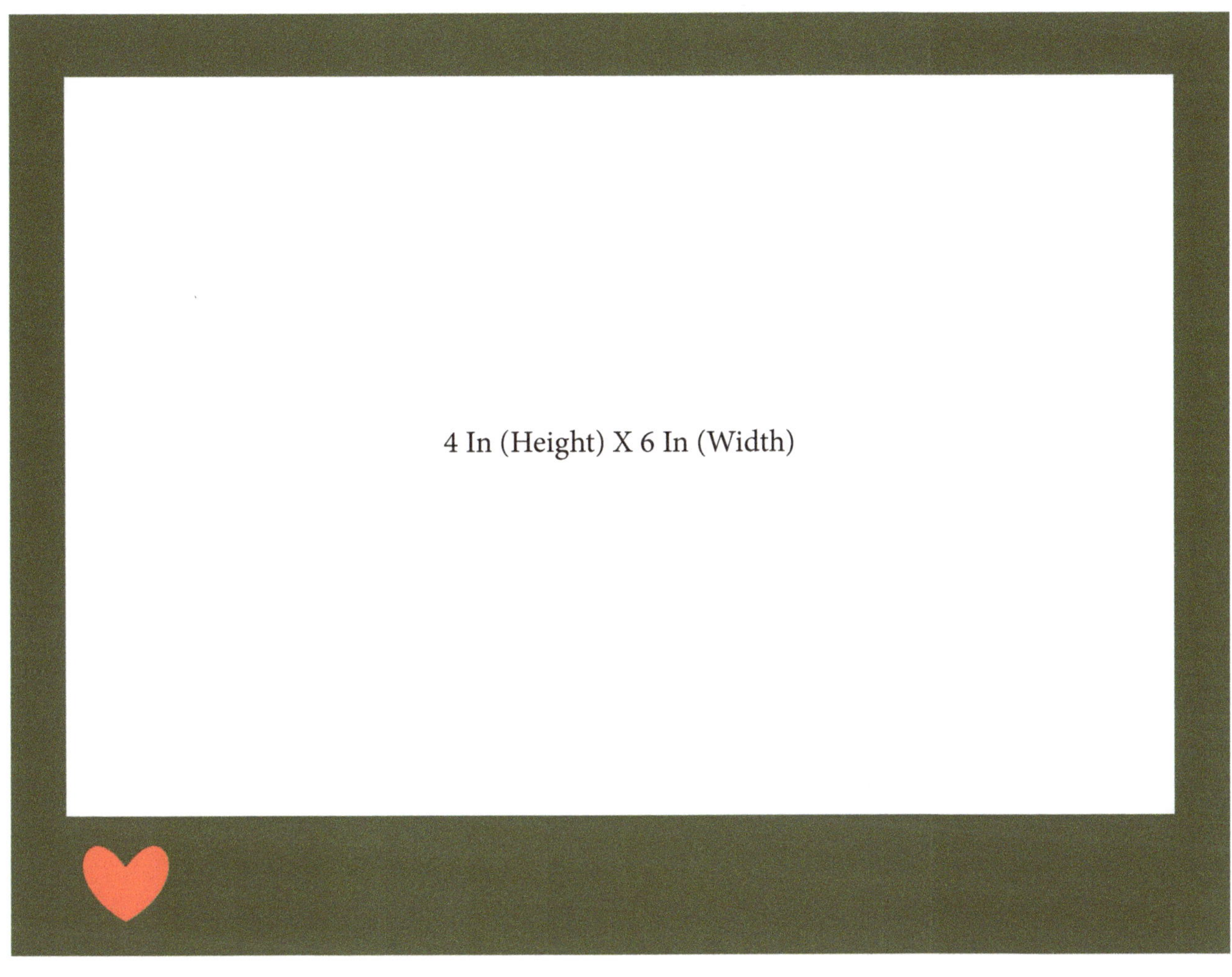

Date:

____
____
____
____
____
____

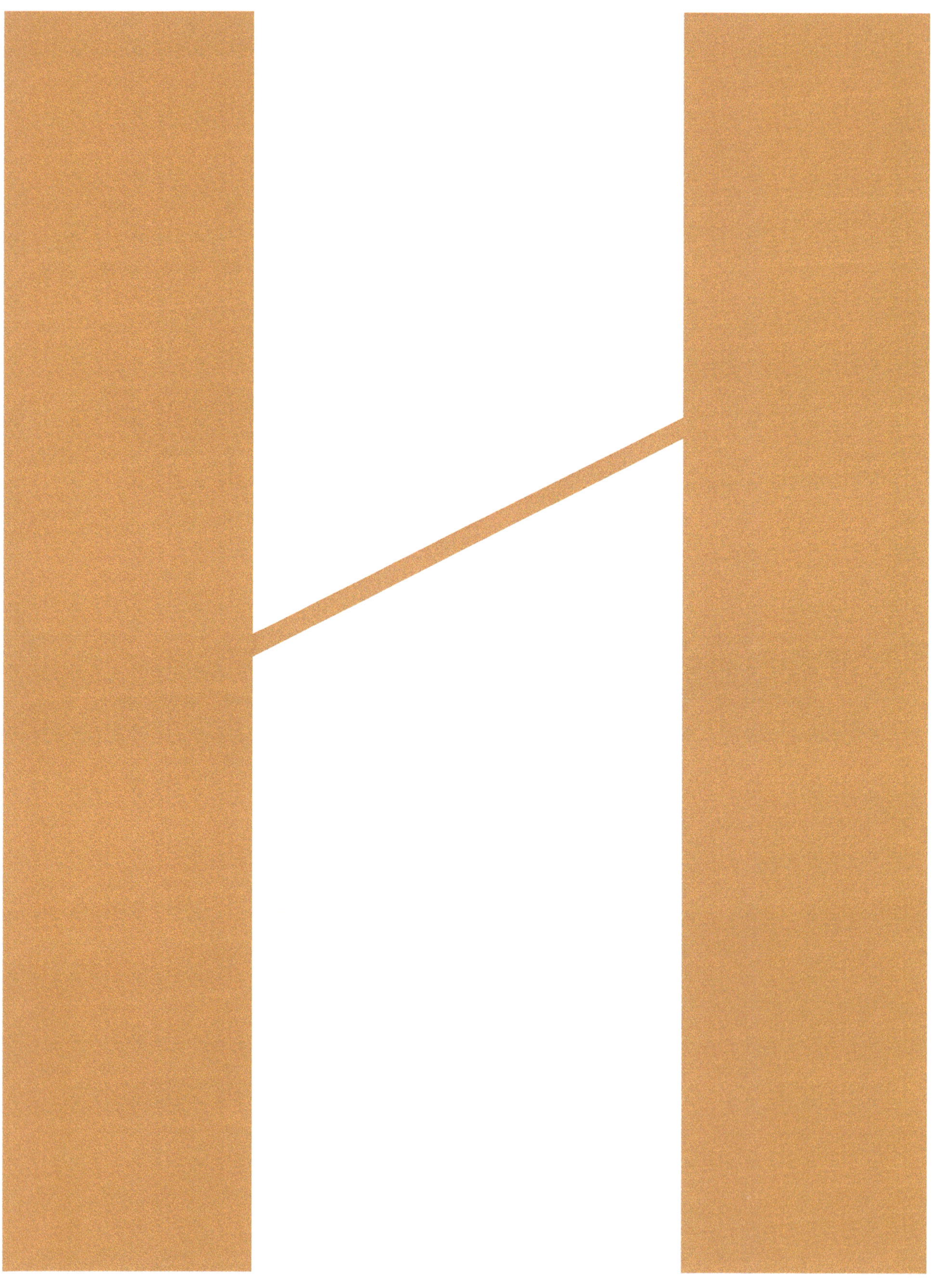

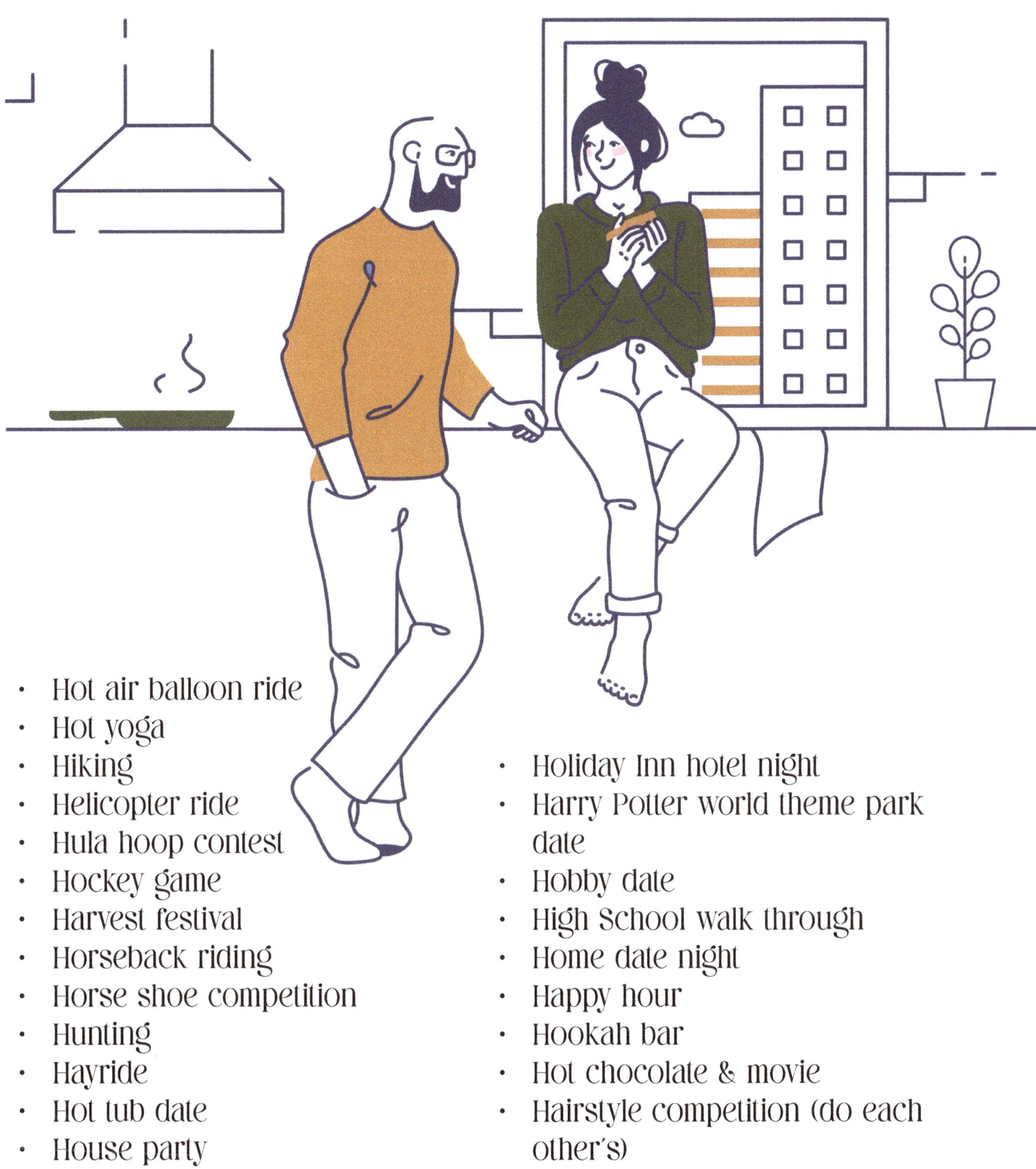

- Hot air balloon ride
- Hot yoga
- Hiking
- Helicopter ride
- Hula hoop contest
- Hockey game
- Harvest festival
- Horseback riding
- Horse shoe competition
- Hunting
- Hayride
- Hot tub date
- House party
- Home decor according to season
- Haunted house
- Holiday Inn hotel night
- Harry Potter world theme park date
- Hobby date
- High School walk through
- Home date night
- Happy hour
- Hookah bar
- Hot chocolate & movie
- Hairstyle competition (do each other's)
- Hulu movie marathon
- Hammock lounging

4 In (Height) X 6 In (Width)

Date:

____
____
____
____
____
____

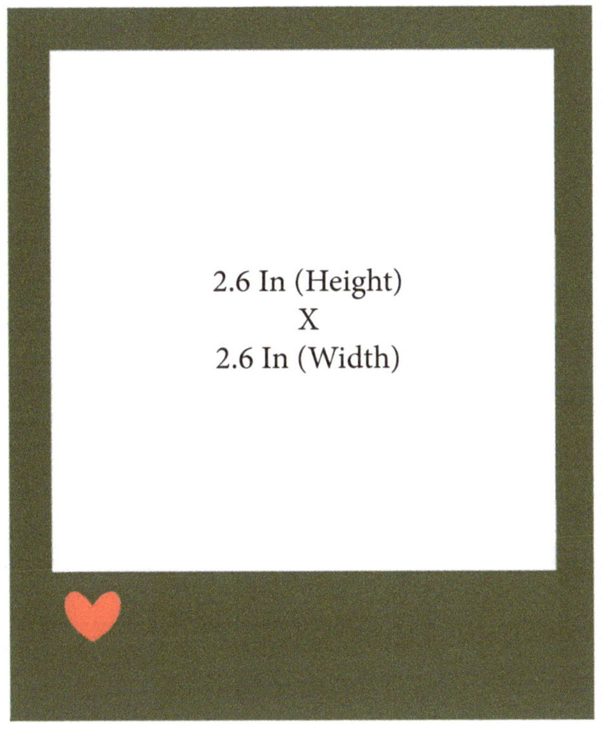

Date:

____
____
____
____
____
____
____

Date:

____
____
____
____
____
____

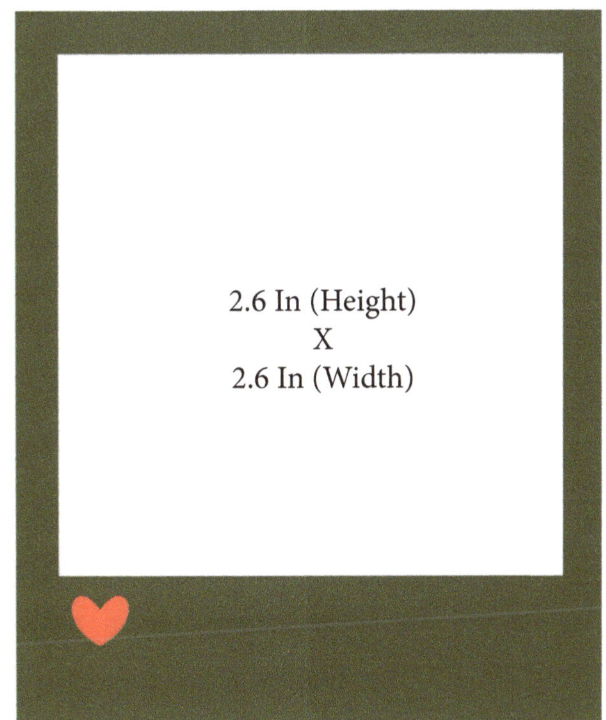

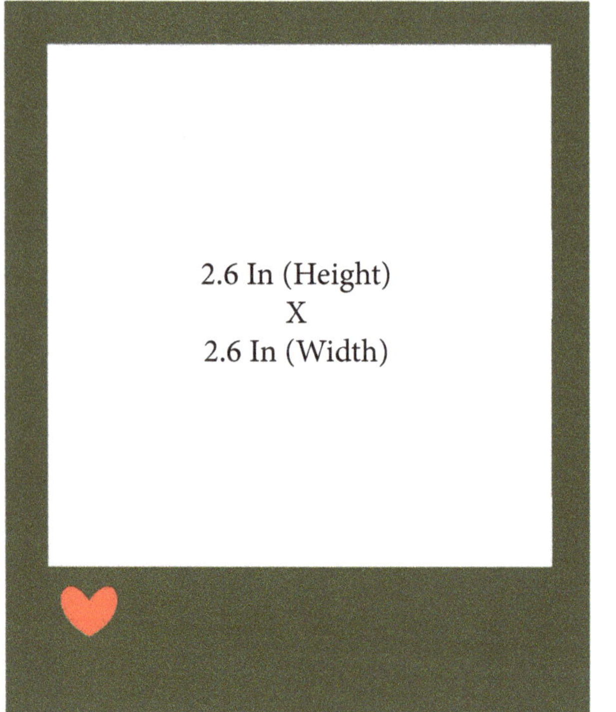

Date:

____
____
____
____
____
____

Date:

____
____
____
____
____
____

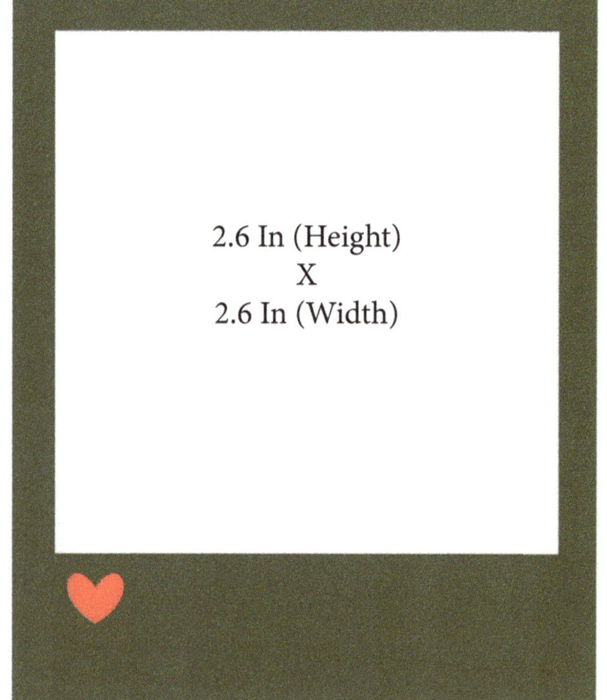

4 In (Height) X 6 In (Width)

Date:

____

____

____

____

____

____

- Ice skating
- Ice cream date
- Indoor camping
- Ice sculpture carving
- Ice bar
- Illusion show
- Improv class
- Imagination date
- Indoor sports game
- Indoor gym workout
- Indoor activities date
- Install something into your home
- Instrumental class
- I-Spy date
- Ink date
- IQ test competition
- Italian ice datev

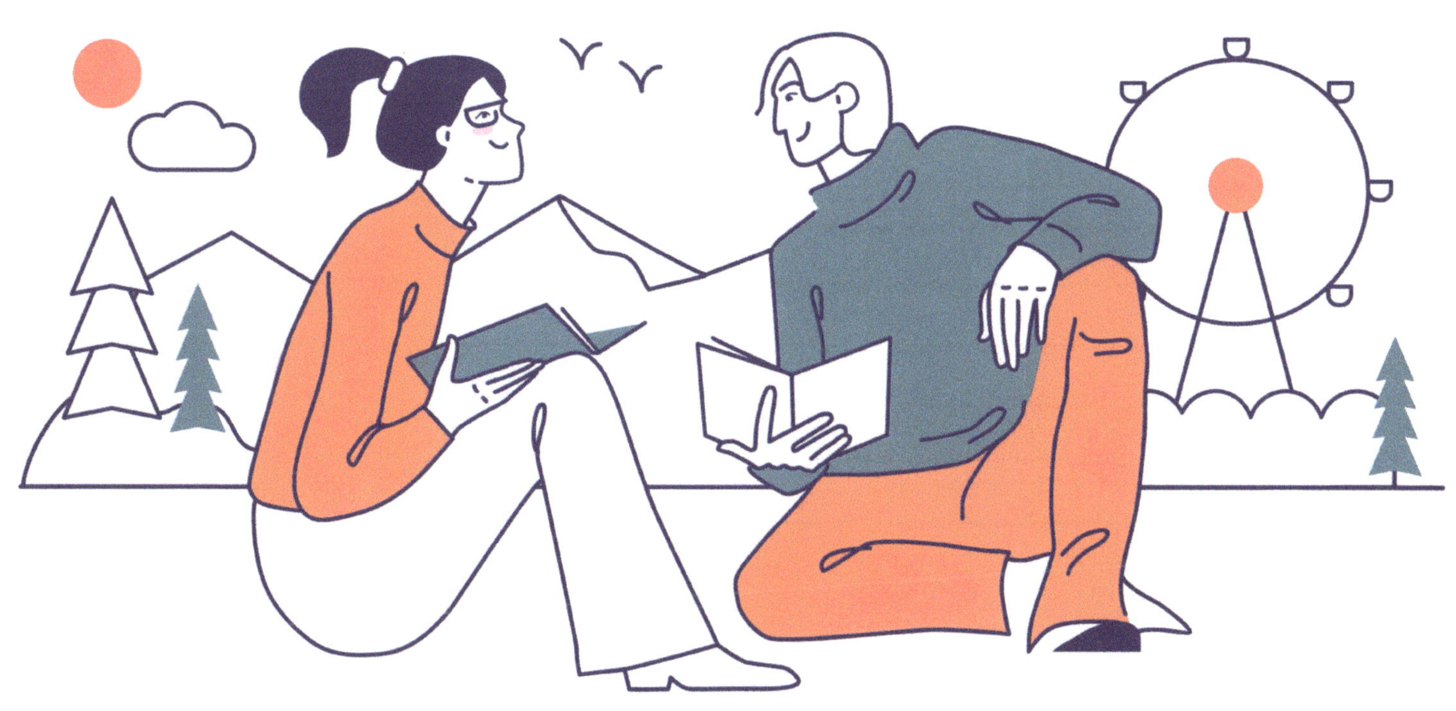

4 In (Height) X 6 In (Width)

Date:

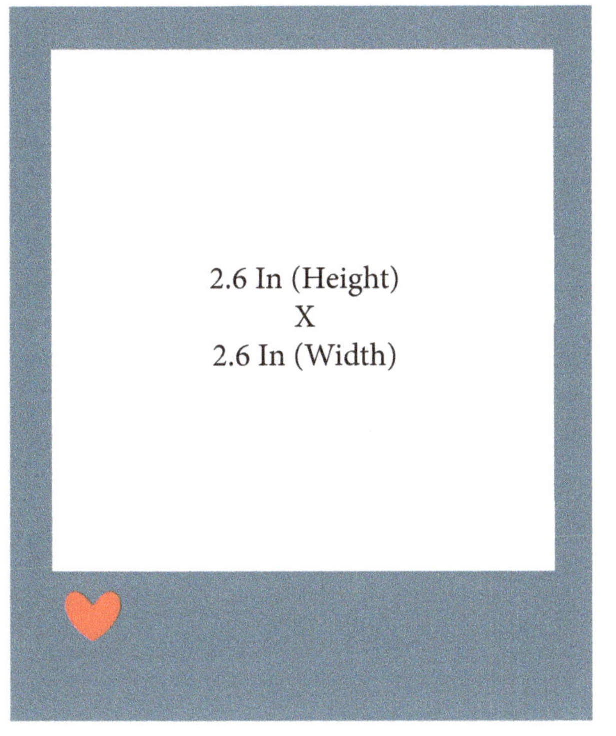

Date:

____
____
____
____
____
____

Date:

____
____
____
____
____
____

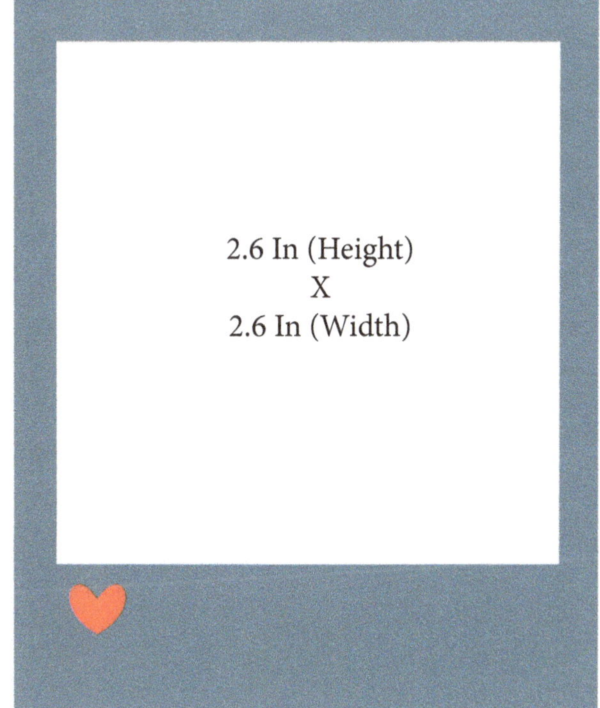

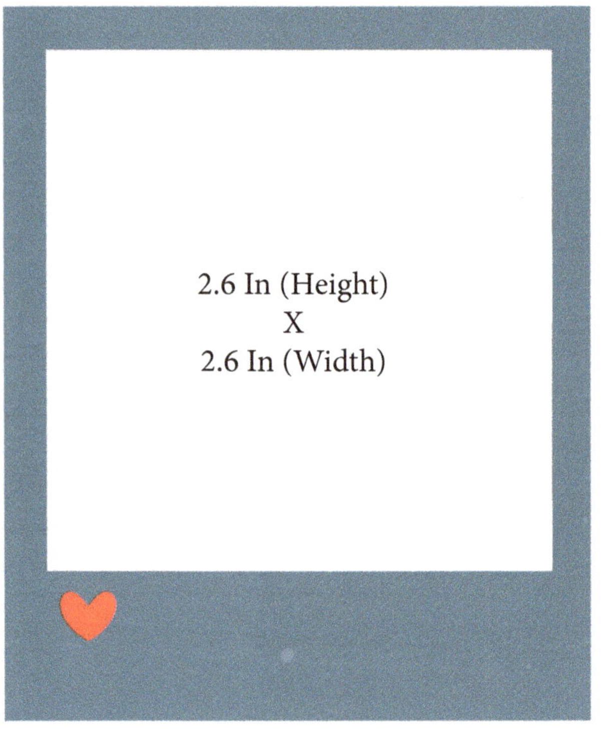

Date:

____

____

____

____

____

____

Date:

____

____

____

____

____

____

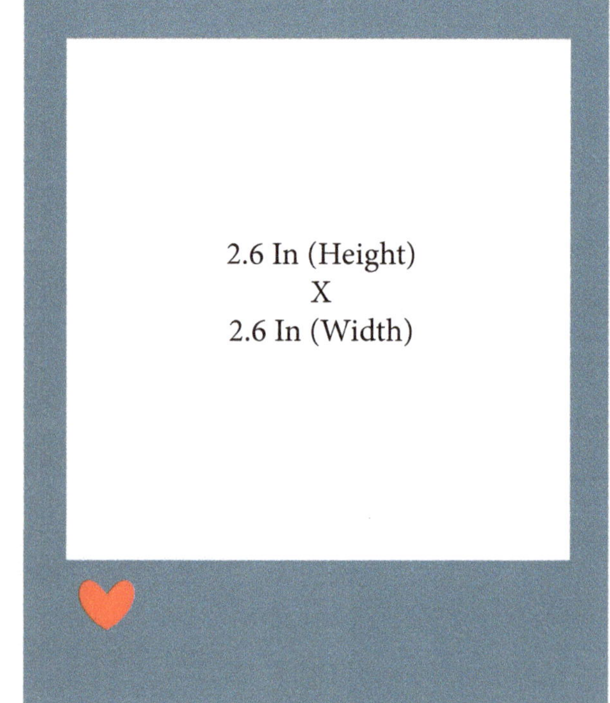

4 In (Height) X 6 In (Width)

Date:
____
____
____
____
____
____

- Jet ski rental
- Jigsaw puzzle
- Jewelry making
- Jog together
- Juggling class
- Journey somewhere new
- Judge a contest
- Jenga date
- Jungle themed date

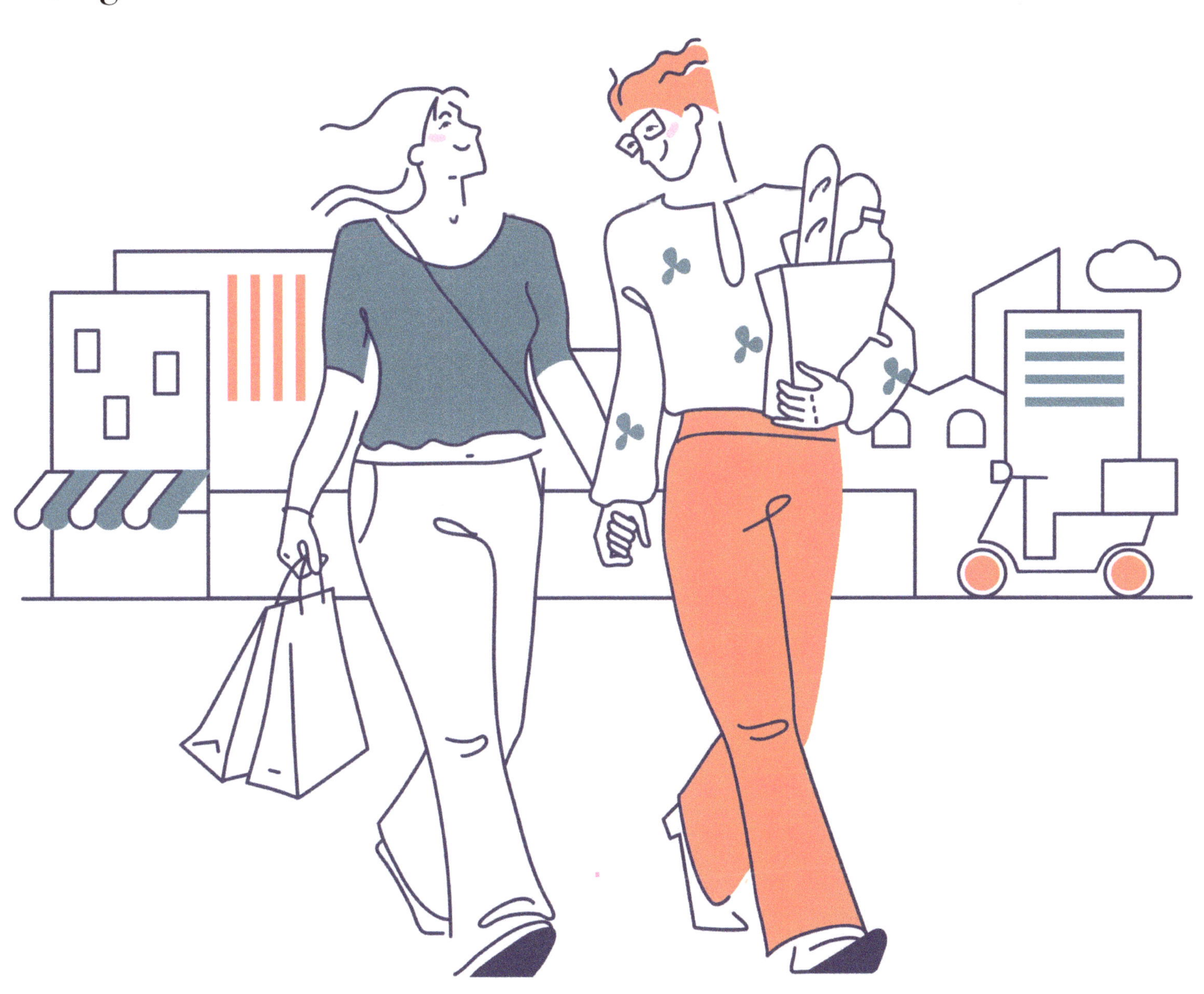

4 In (Height) X 6 In (Width)

Date:

2.6 In (Height)
X
2.6 In (Width)

Date:

Date:

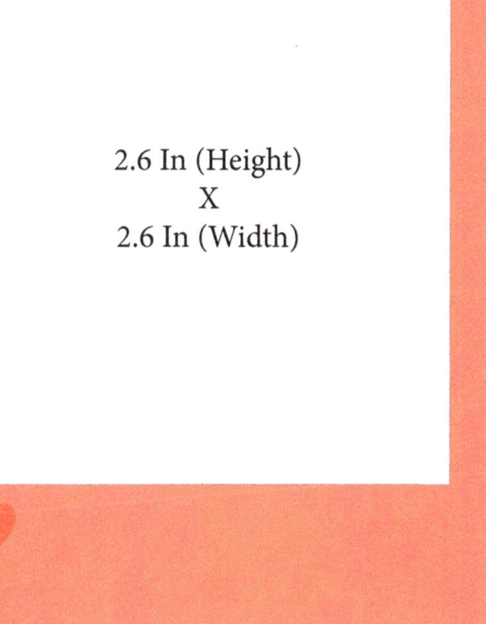

2.6 In (Height)
X
2.6 In (Width)

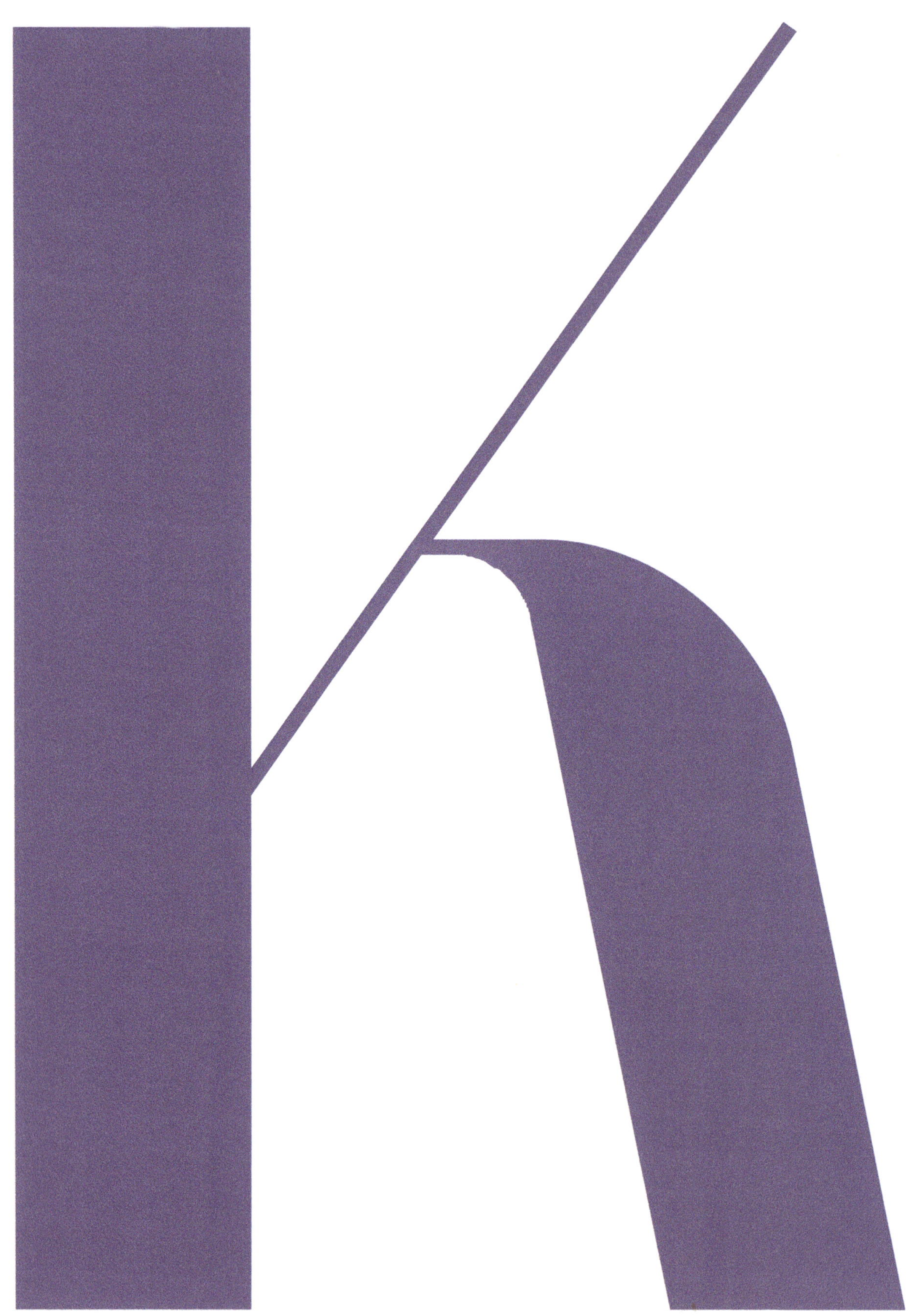

- Karaoke
- Kickboxing
- Kayaking
- Kite flying
- Karate class
- Knitting class
- Kentucky Derby
- King for a day
- Kale sunset

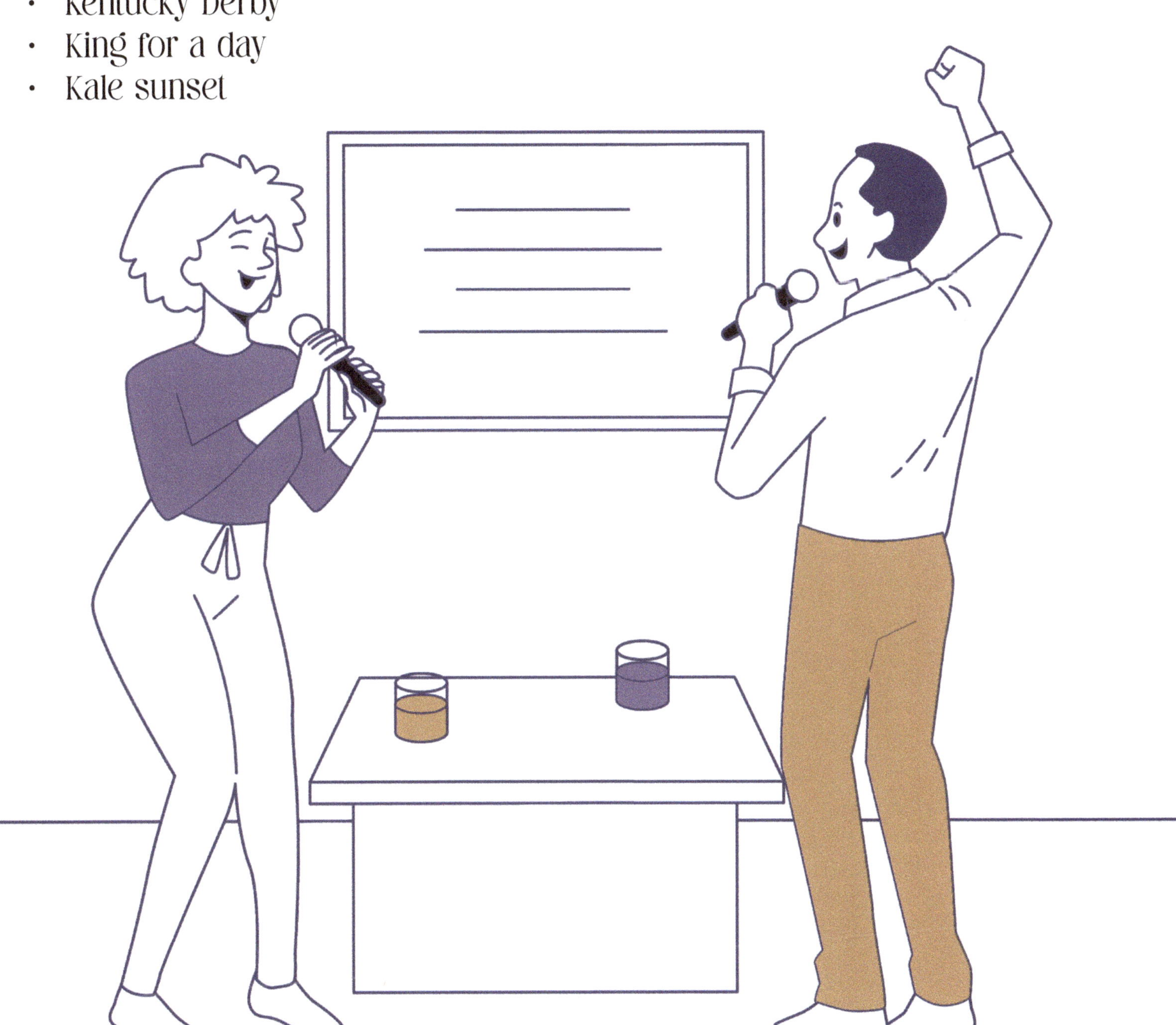

4 In (Height) X 6 In (Width)

Date:
____
____
____
____
____
____

2.6 In (Height)
X
2.6 In (Width)

Date:

Date:

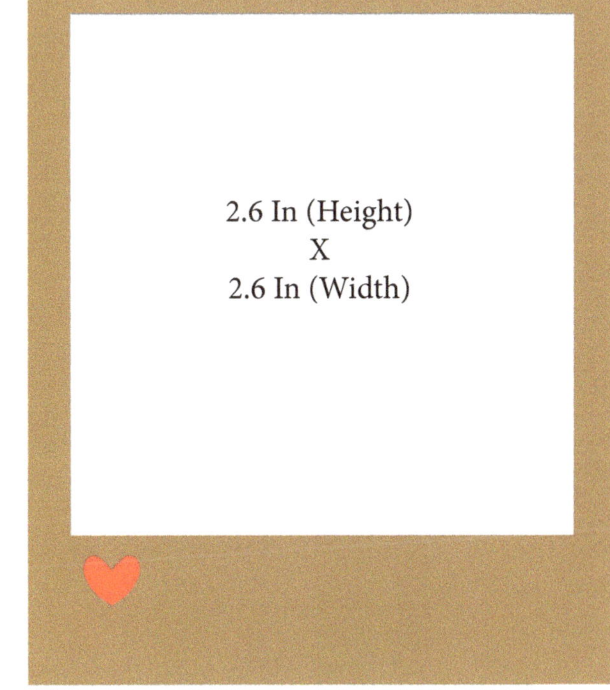

2.6 In (Height)
X
2.6 In (Width)

- Limousine ride
- Line dancing
- Local pub crawl
- Long walk
- Love letter exchange
- Laser tag
- Light show
- Limo ride
- Learn something new
- Live music/band concert
- Line dancing class
- Library date
- Legoland
- Local adventure
- Lodge cabin getaway
- Lottery drawing
- Luxury lunch
- Lightshowv

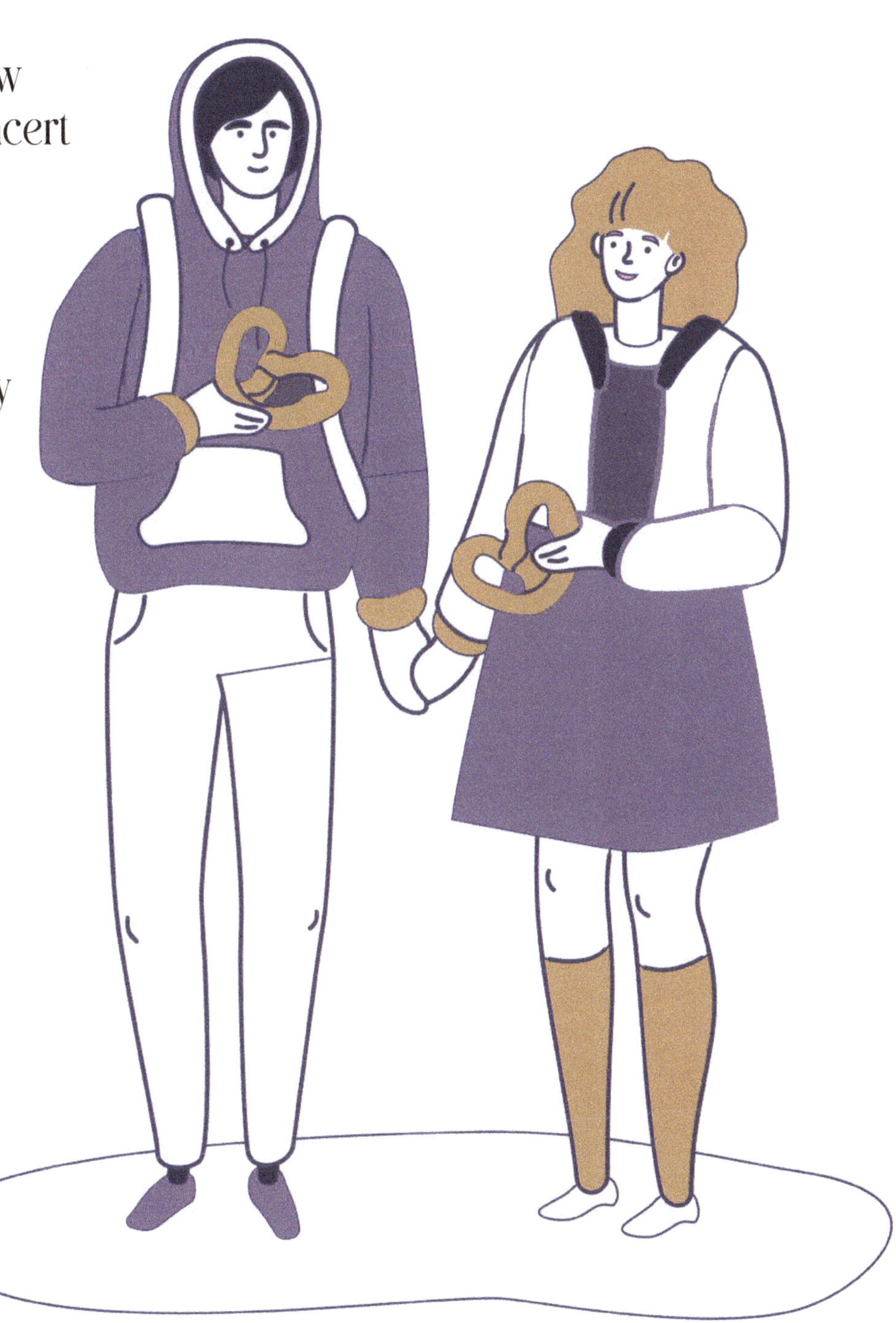

4 In (Height) X 6 In (Width)

Date:

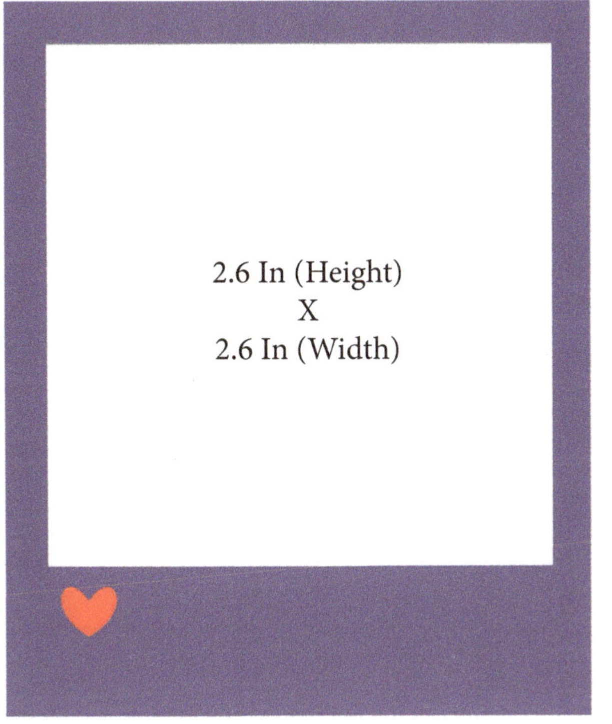

Date:

____

____

____

____

____

____

Date:

____

____

____

____

____

____

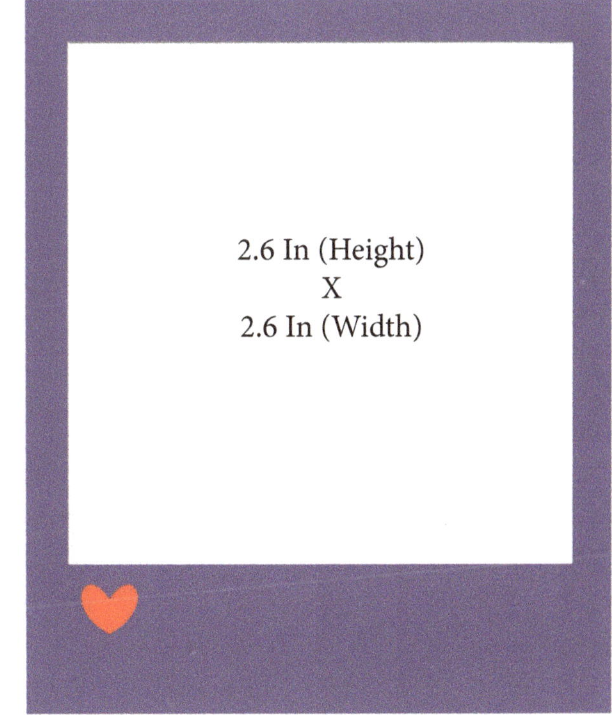

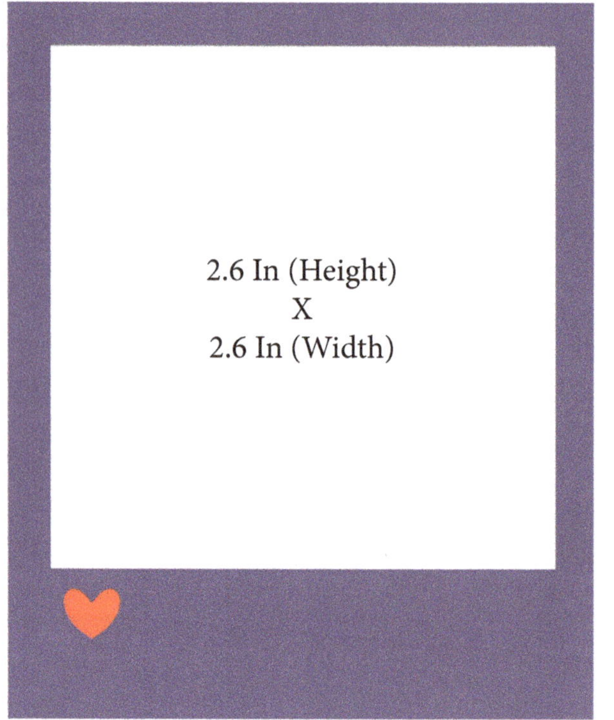

Date:

____

____

____

____

____

____

Date:

____

____

____

____

____

____

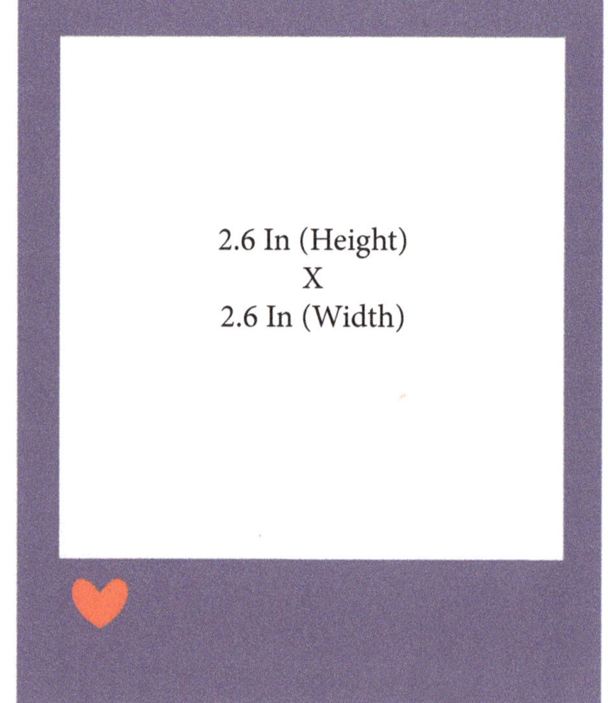

4 In (Height) X 6 In (Width)

Date:

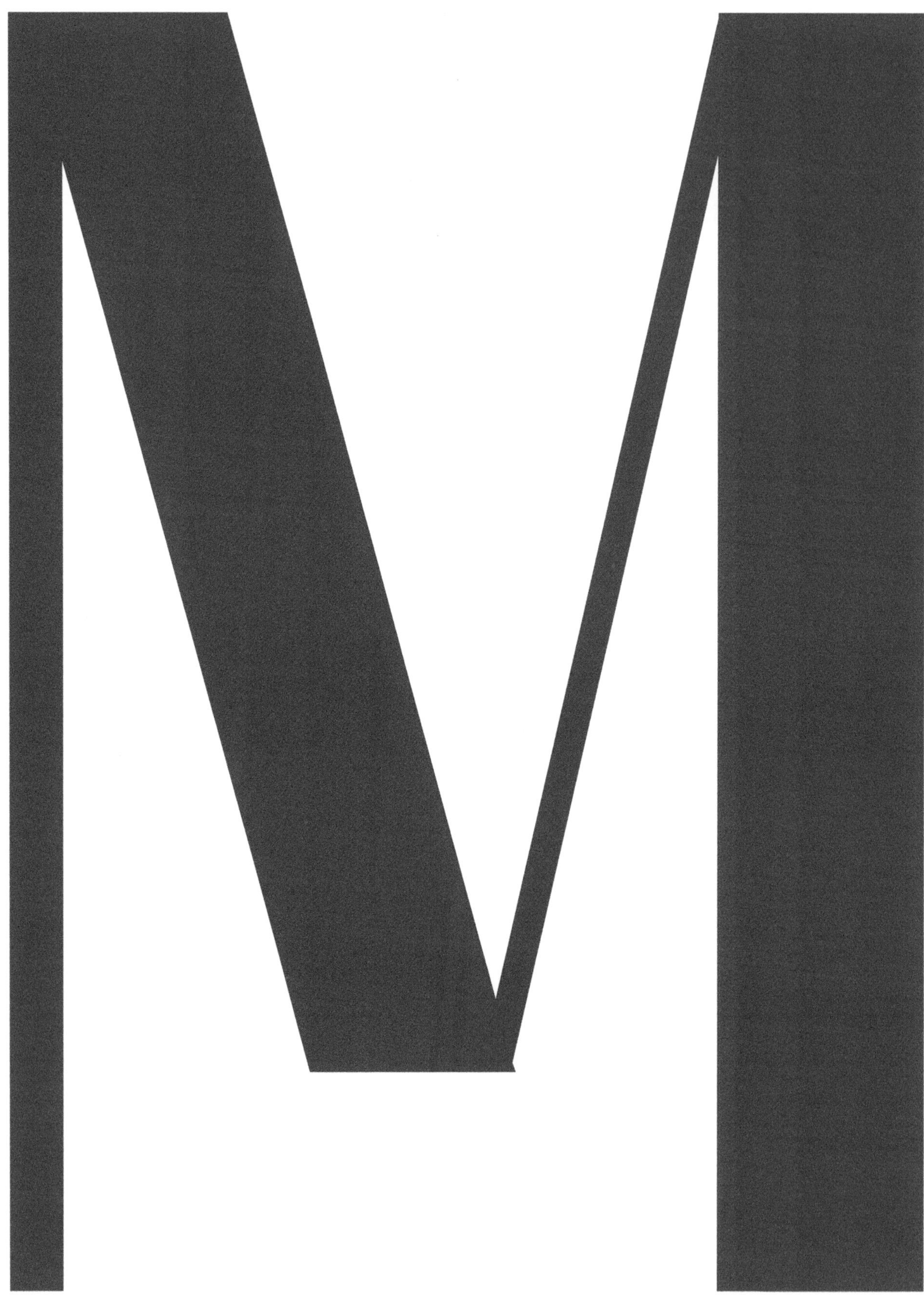

- Mixology lessons
- Mini-golf
- Massages exchange
- Murder mystery show/movie
- Murder mystery board game
- Movie night
- Music concert
- Magic show
- Movie & a meal
- Meteor shower
- Morning date
- Marshmallow roasting
- Monopoly game night

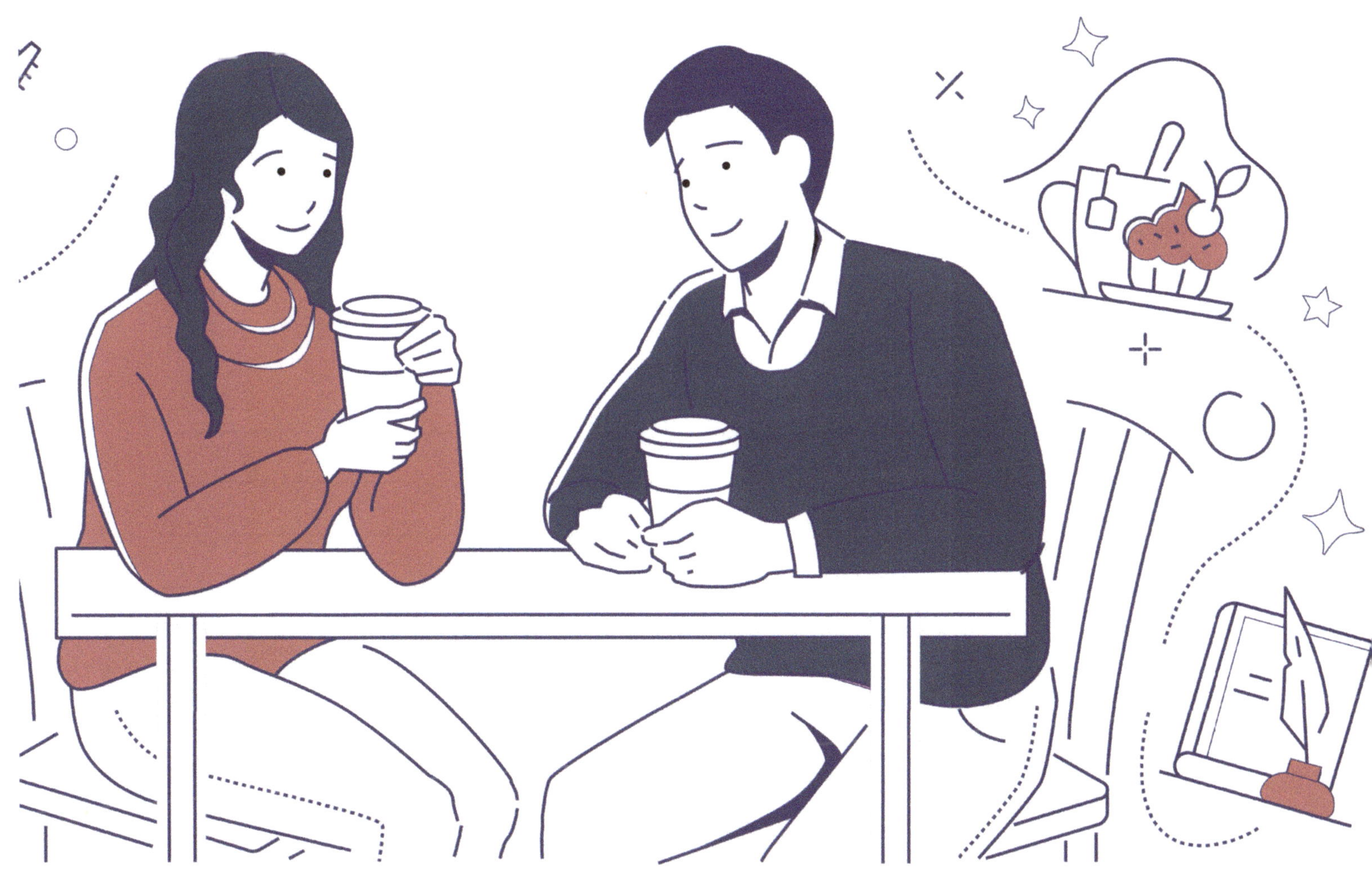

4 In (Height) X 6 In (Width)

Date:

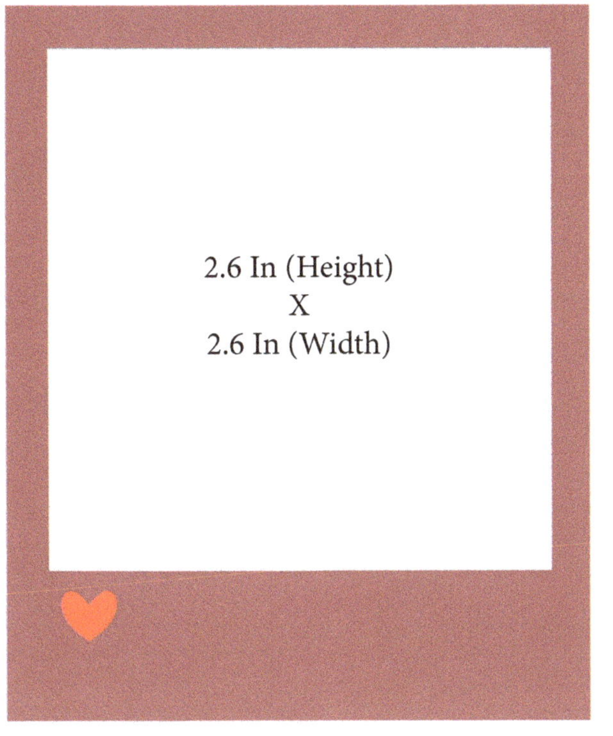

Date:

____

____

____

____

____

____

Date:

____

____

____

____

____

____

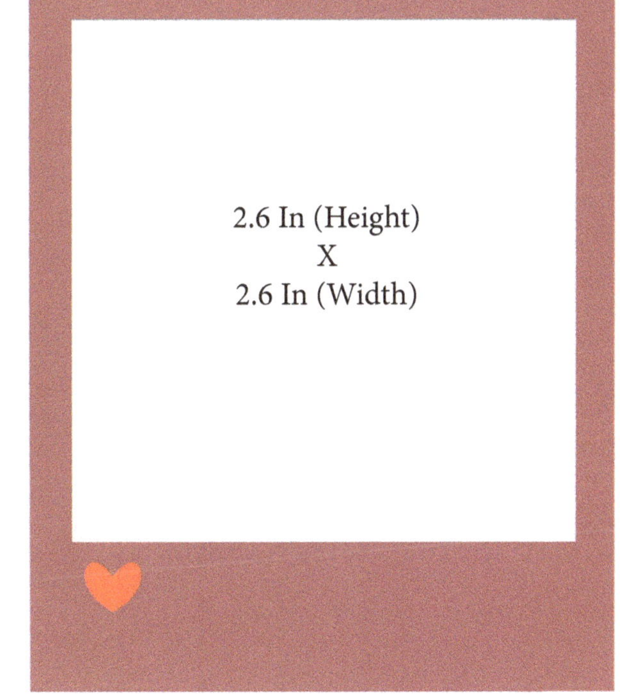

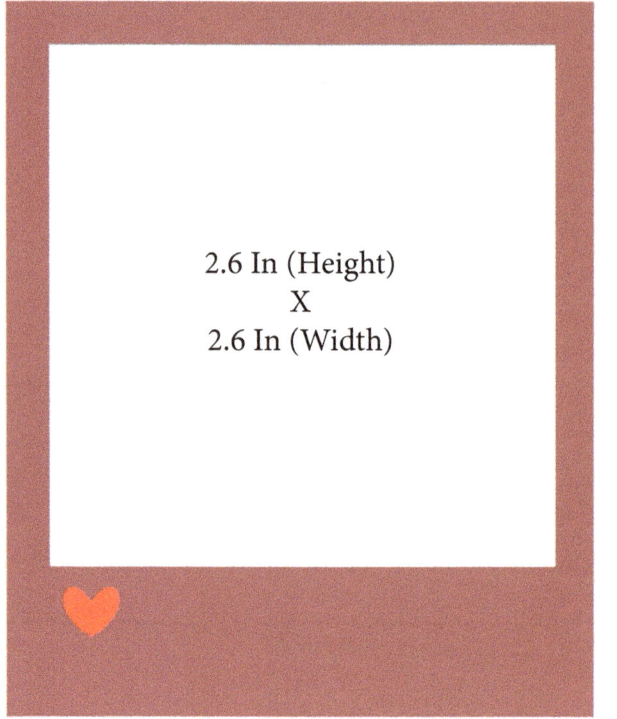

Date:

____

____

____

____

____

____

Date:

____

____

____

____

____

____

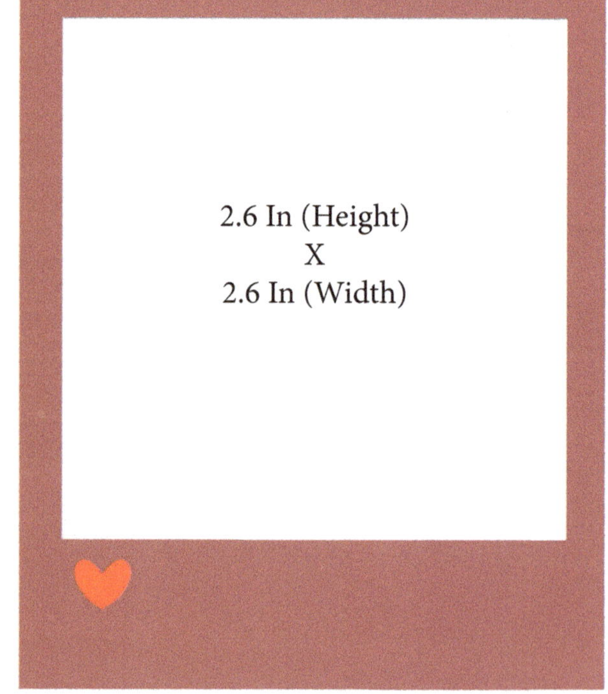

4 In (Height) X 6 In (Width)

Date:

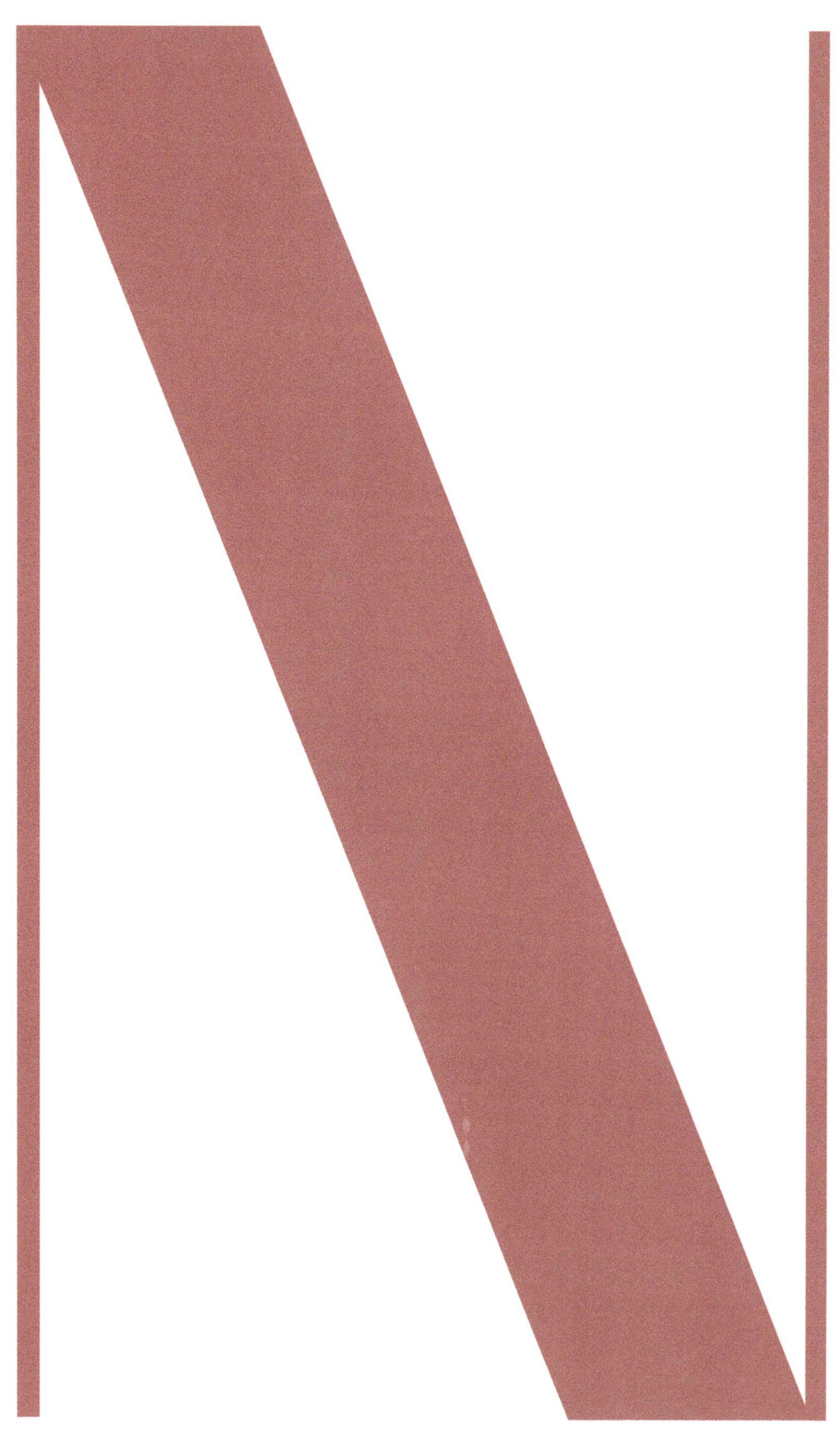

- Nacho-night
- Nature walk
- Nightclubbing
- Netflix-binge watch
- National park visit
- Nature walk
- Nature scavenger hunt
- NFL Football game
- NBA Basketball game
- Niagara Falls
- Norther lights
- Noah's Ark
- Neon date
- Nursey planning
- Netflix roulette
- Nerf gun war
- Night Date of your choice

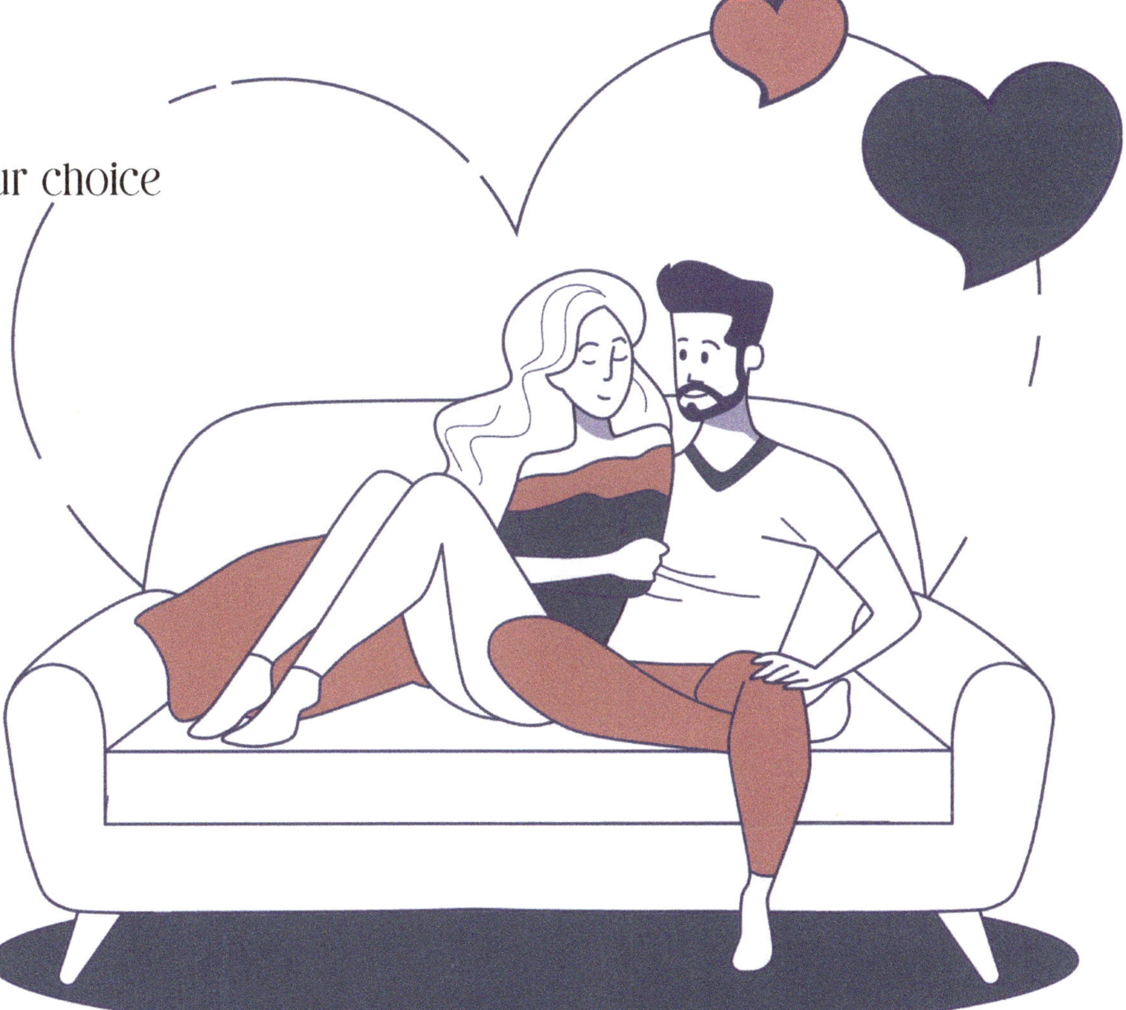

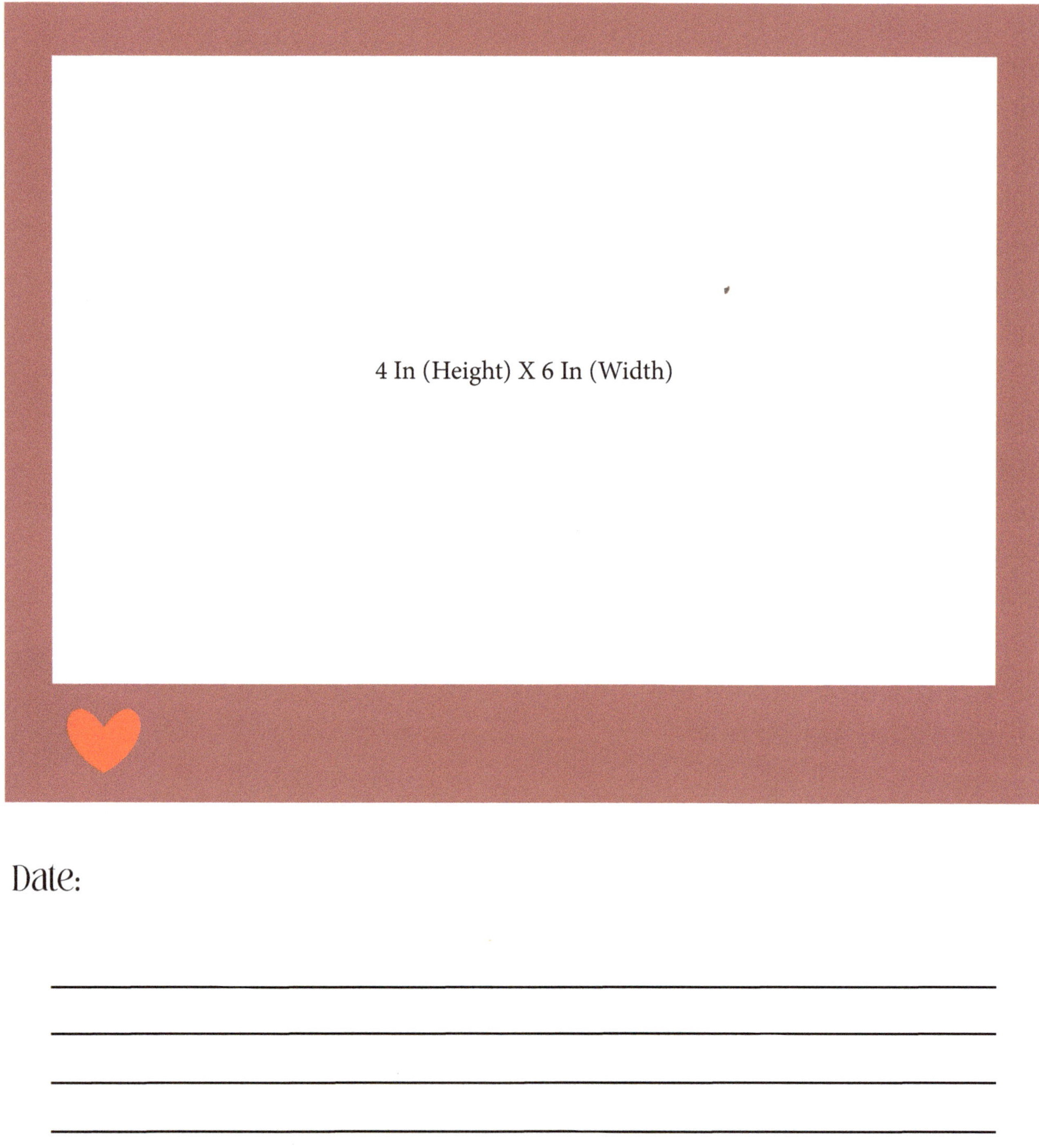

Date:

____
____
____
____
____
____

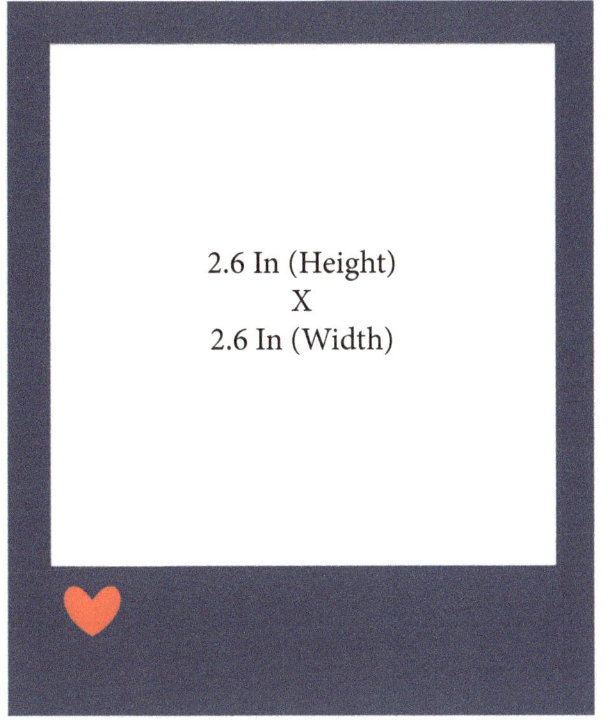

Date:

____
____
____
____
____
____

Date:

____
____
____
____
____
____

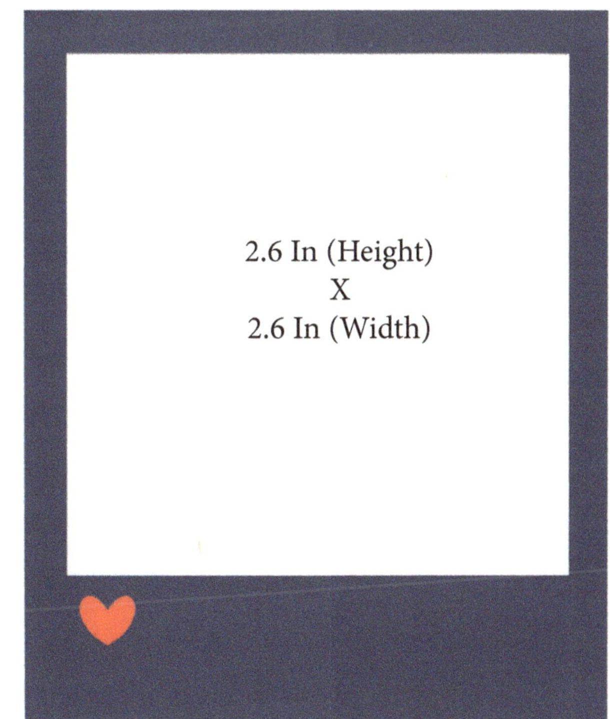

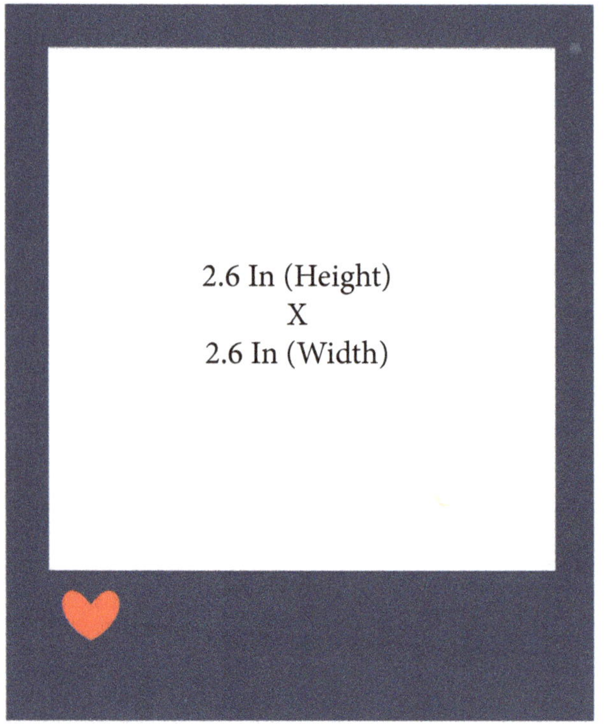

Date:

____
____
____
____
____
____

Date:

____
____
____
____
____
____

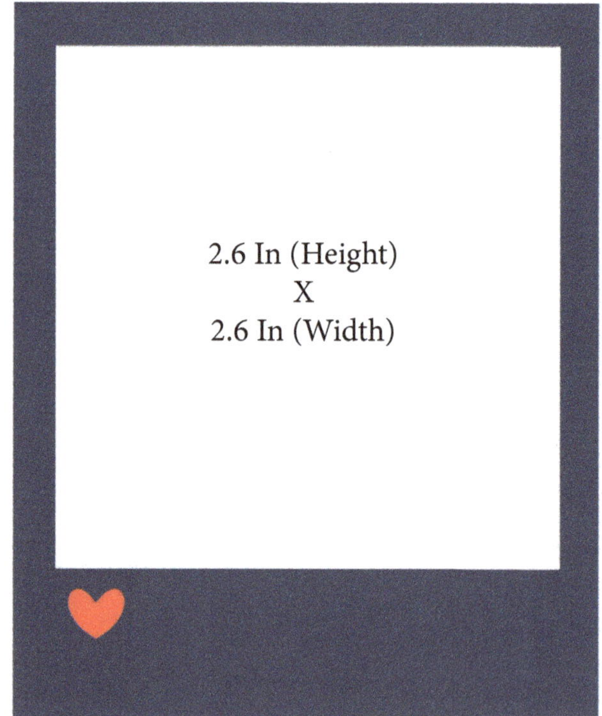

4 In (Height) X 6 In (Width)

Date:

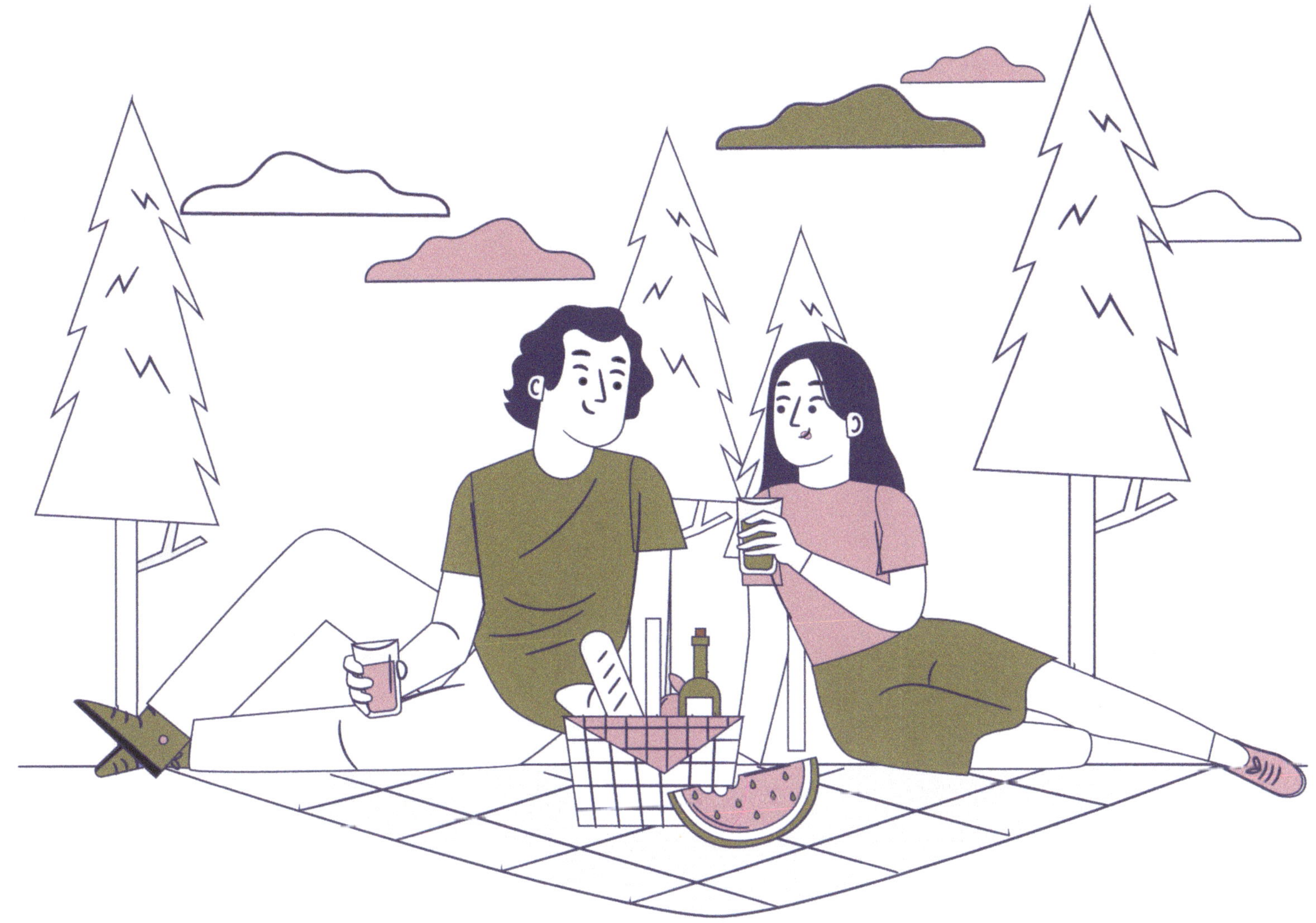

- Origami
- Off-roading
- Orchestra concert
- Ocean watching
- Orchard visit
- Orange picking
- Old photos exchange
- Outdoor date of your choice
- Open range shooting'
- Open range golfing
- Organize something in your house
- Opposite date
- Orby gun battle
- Obstacle course
- Omelets breakfast

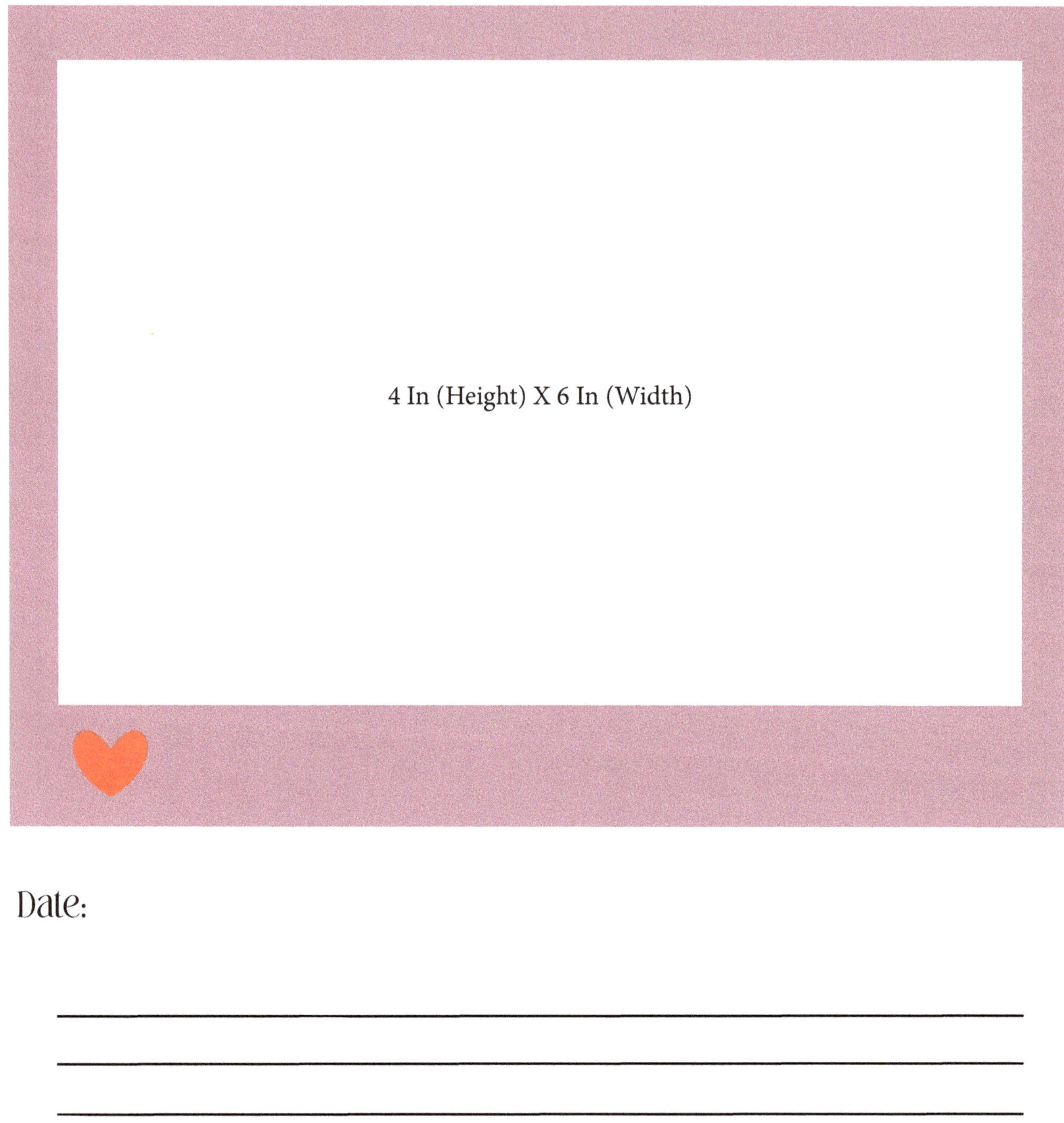

Date:

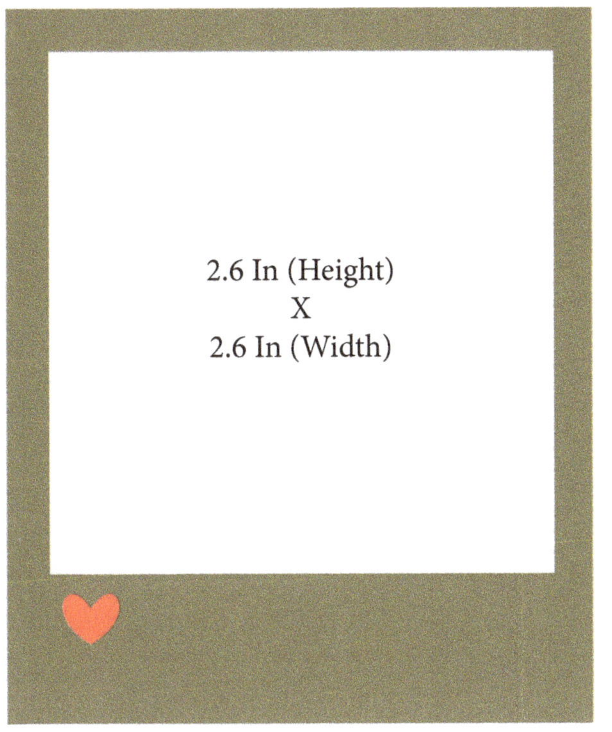

Date:

____
____
____
____
____
____

Date:

____
____
____
____
____
____

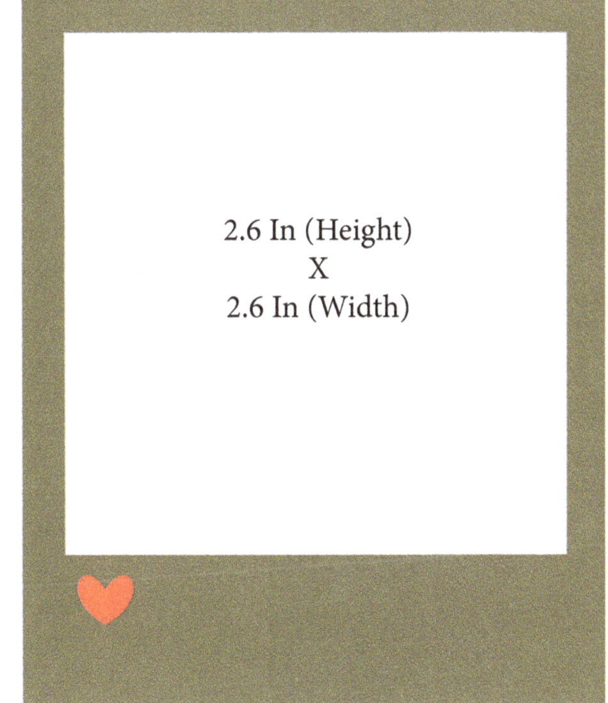

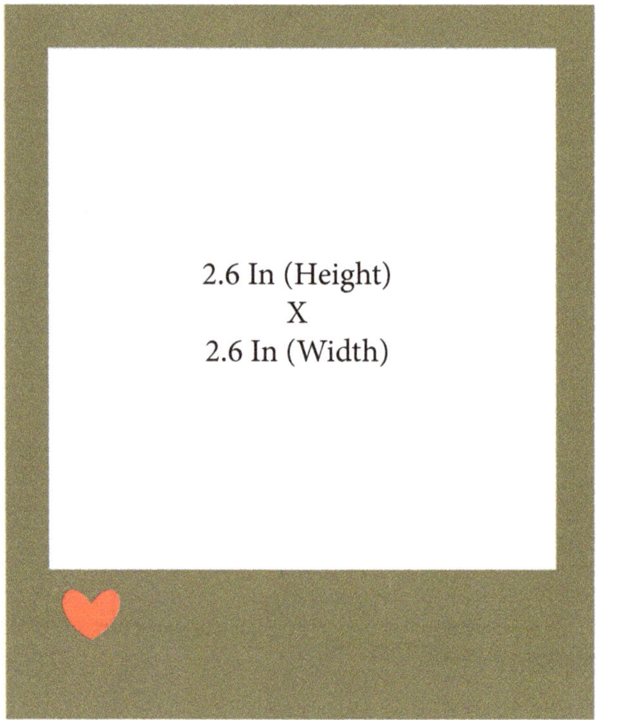

Date:

____

____

____

____

____

____

Date:

____

____

____

____

____

____

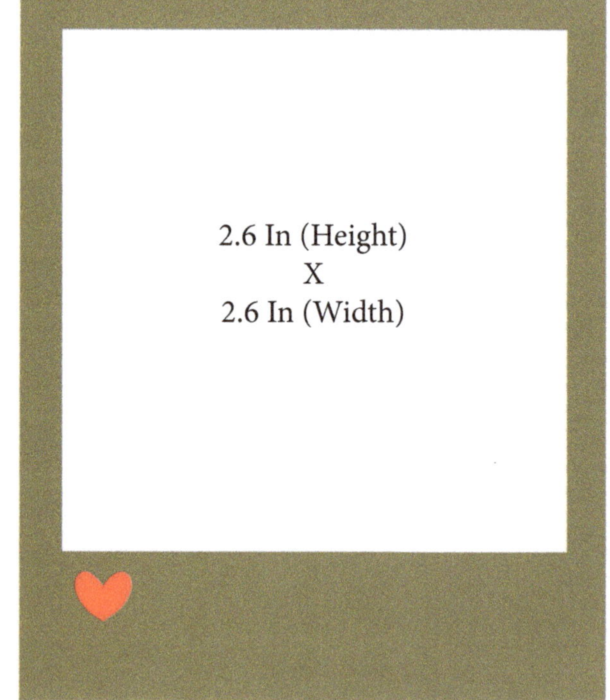

4 In (Height) X 6 In (Width)

Date:

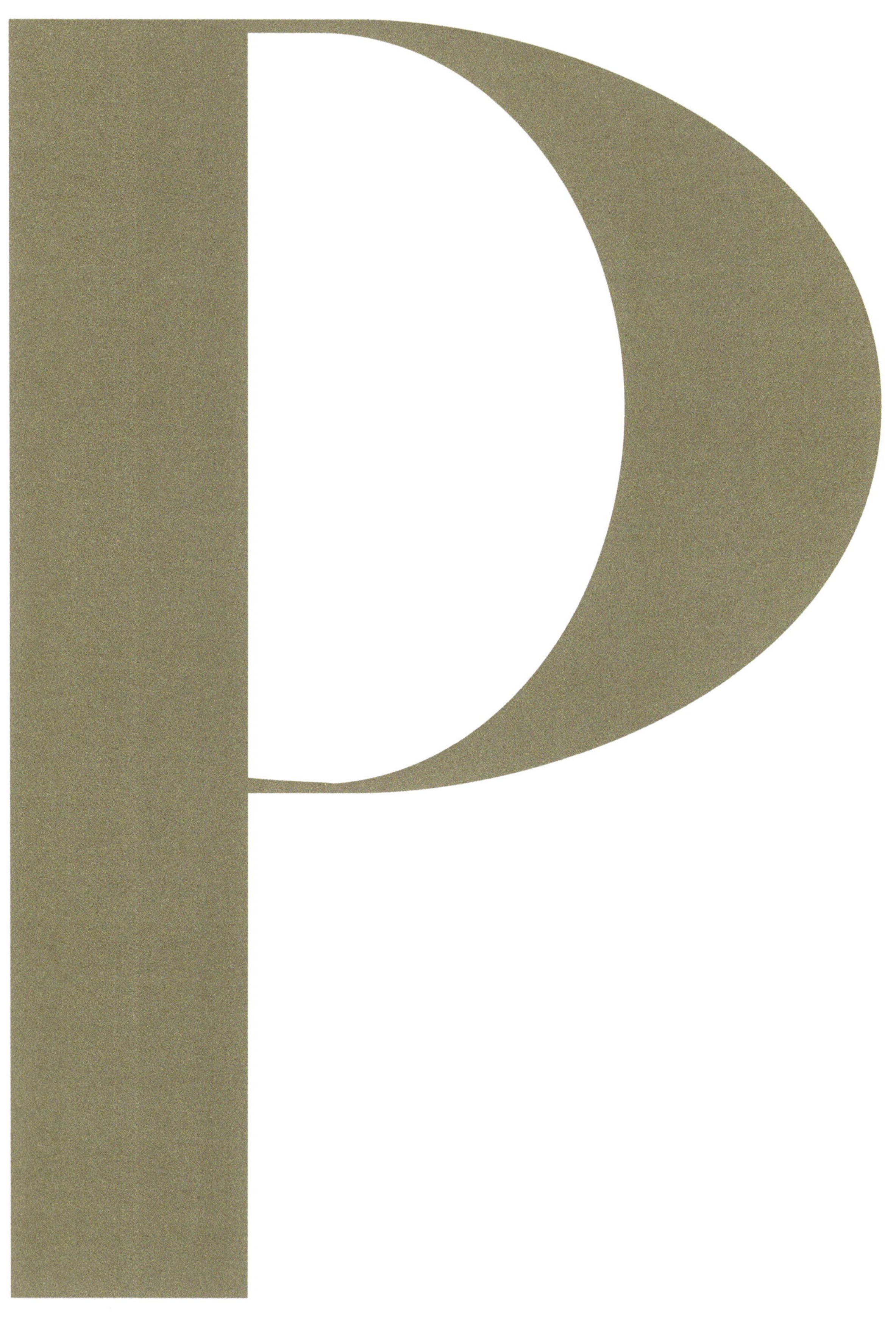

- Paint and sip
- Pottery painting
- Private boat cruise
- Picnic in the park
- Planetarium
- Pool float movie night
- Party
- Petting zoo
- Picnic
- Putt Putt gold
- Painting class
- Paintball
- Parade
- Park visit
- Pottery classes
- Pinterest Project
- Photoshoot
- Paddle Boat date
- Plant a tree
- Polar Bear plunge
- Pajama day
- Pumpkin patch
- Prince/princess themed date
- Pillsbury date
- Popcorn & movie night
- Pickleball

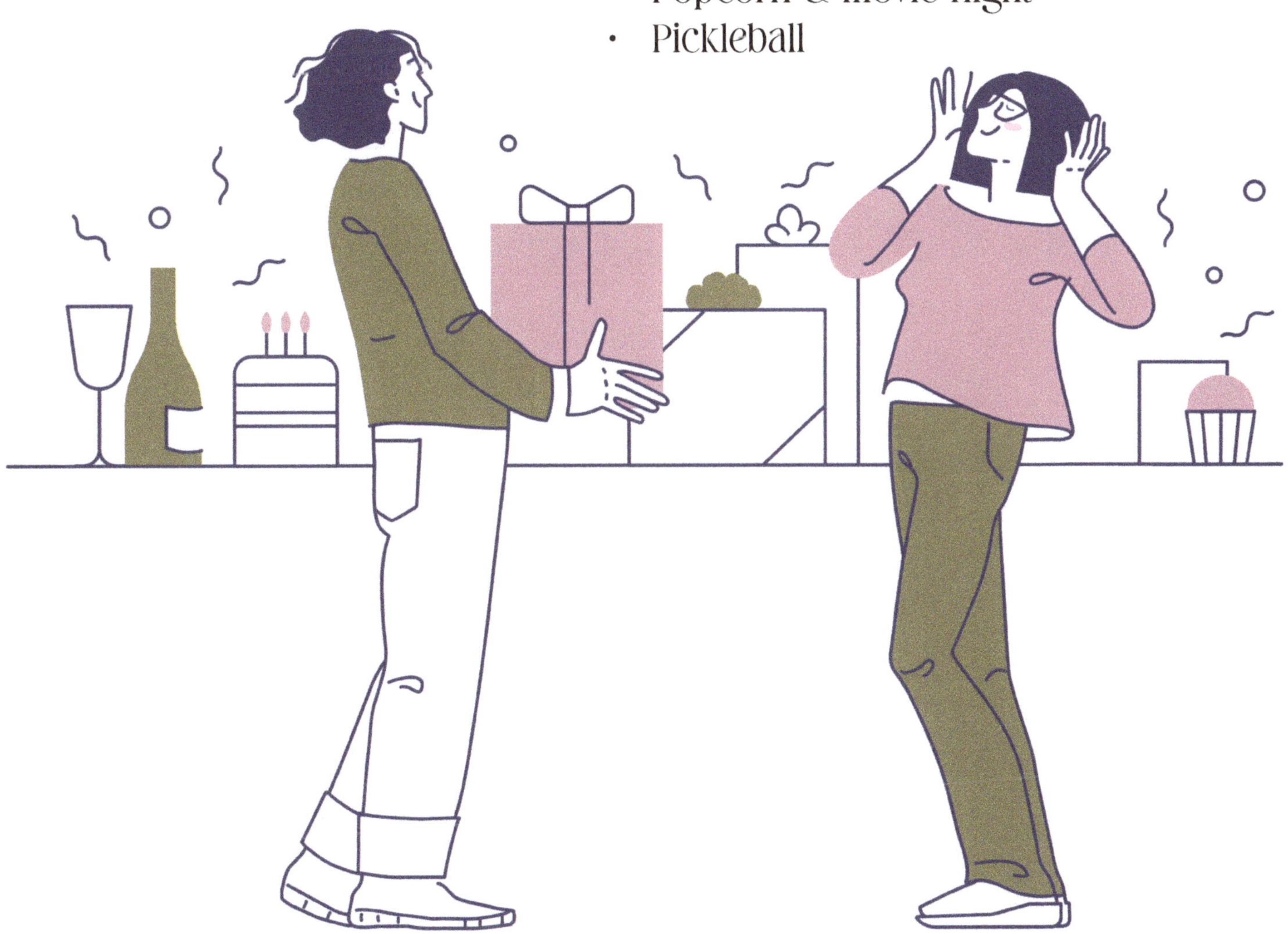

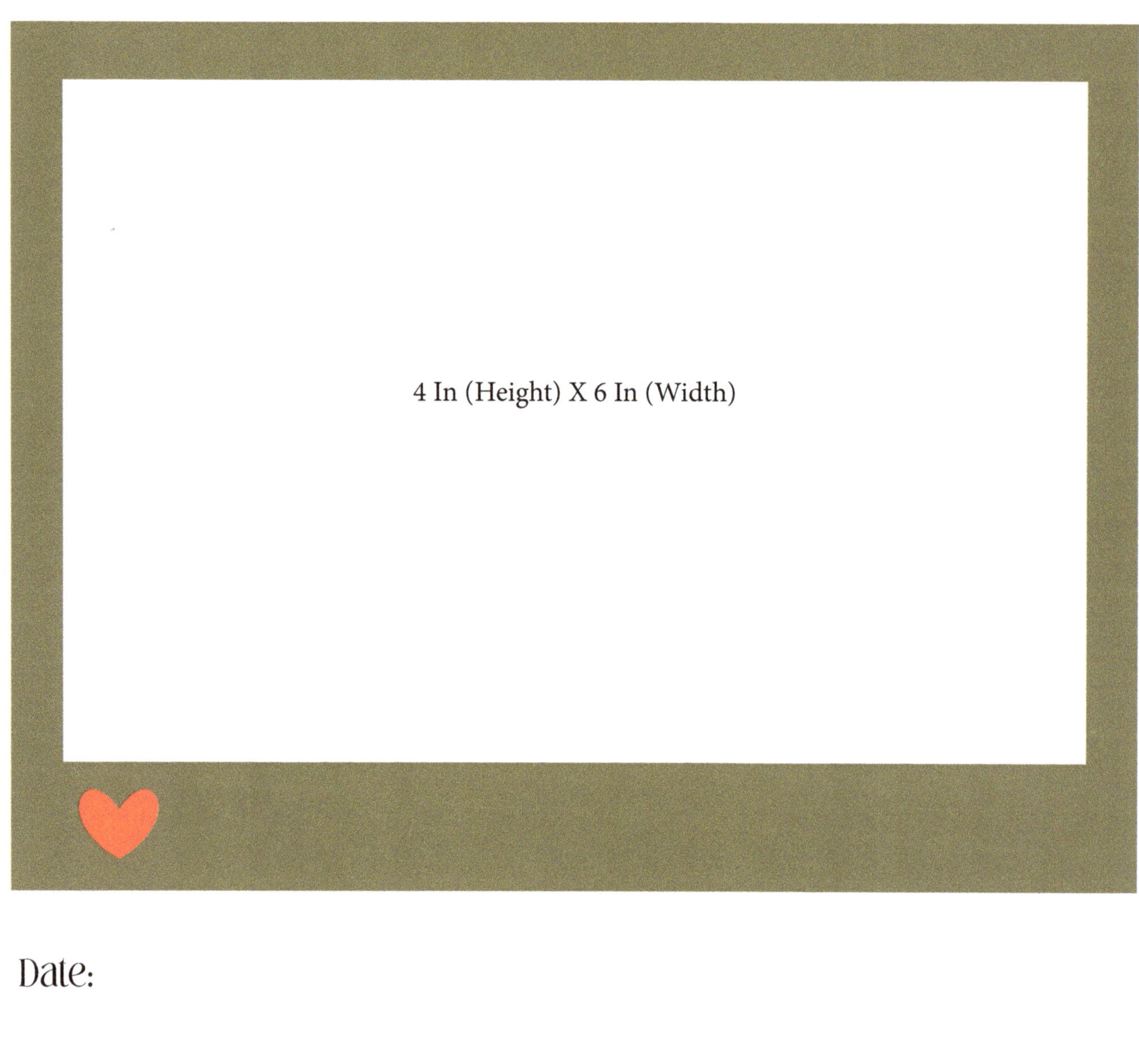

Date:
____
____
____
____
____
____

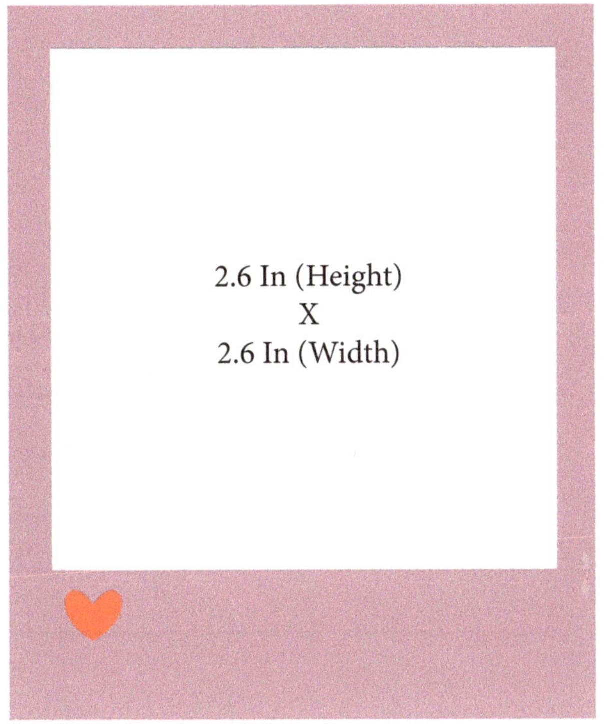

Date:

____

____

____

____

____

____

Date:

____

____

____

____

____

____

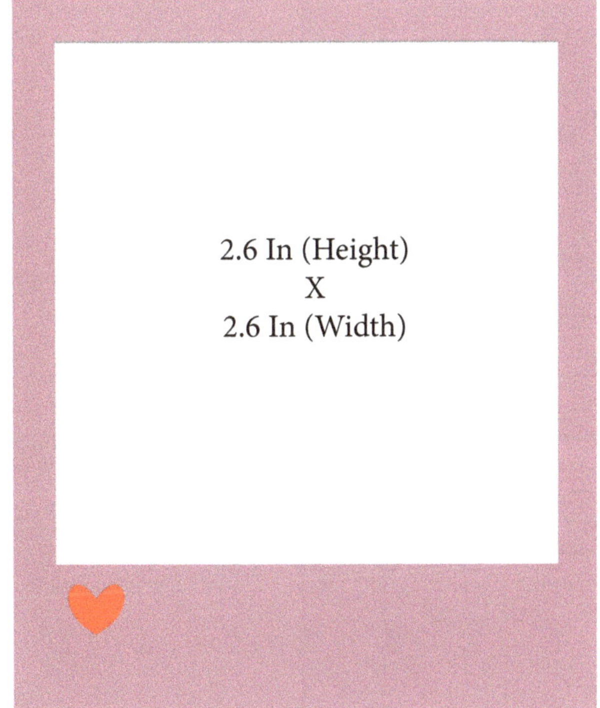

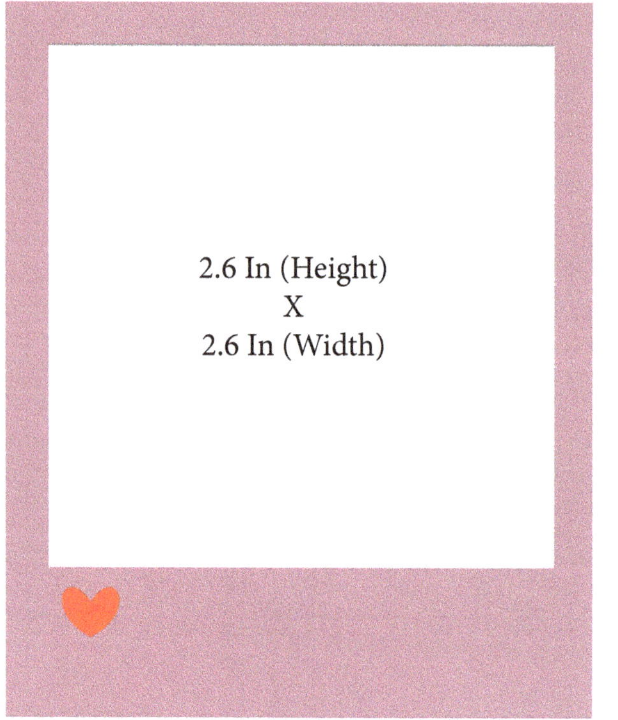

Date:

____

____

____

____

____

____

Date:

____

____

____

____

____

____

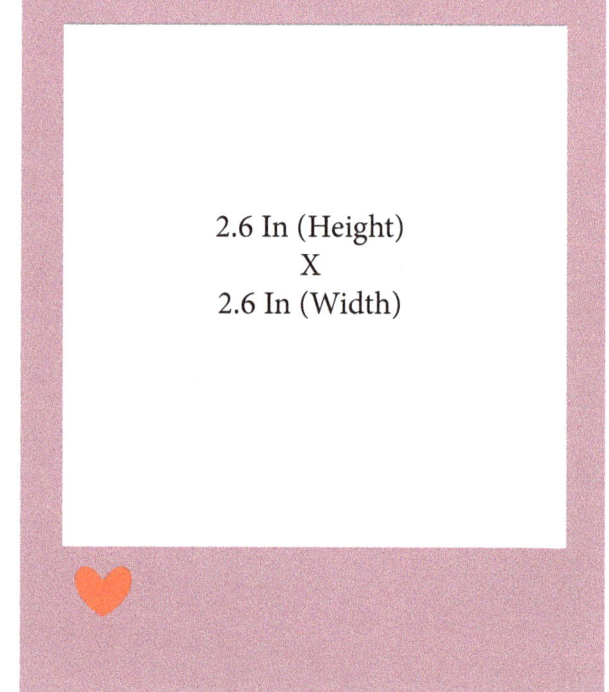

4 In (Height) X 6 In (Width)

Date:

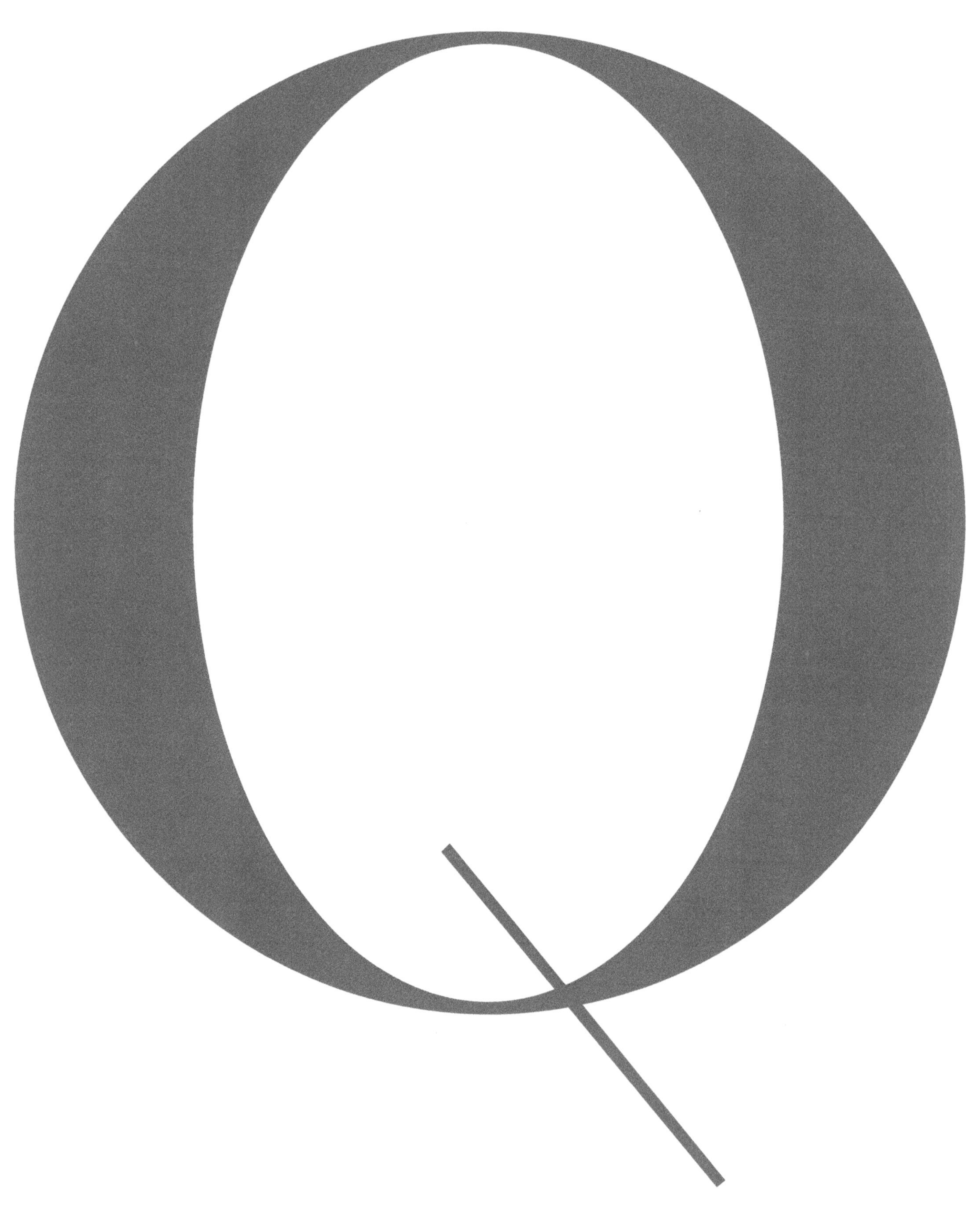

- Quiet dinner for two at a restaurant
- Quiet dinner for two at-home style
- Quick trip out of town
- Quilt making
- Quiz each other
- Quote a movie line, guess the movie
- Quadruple date
- Questions game
- Queen for the day

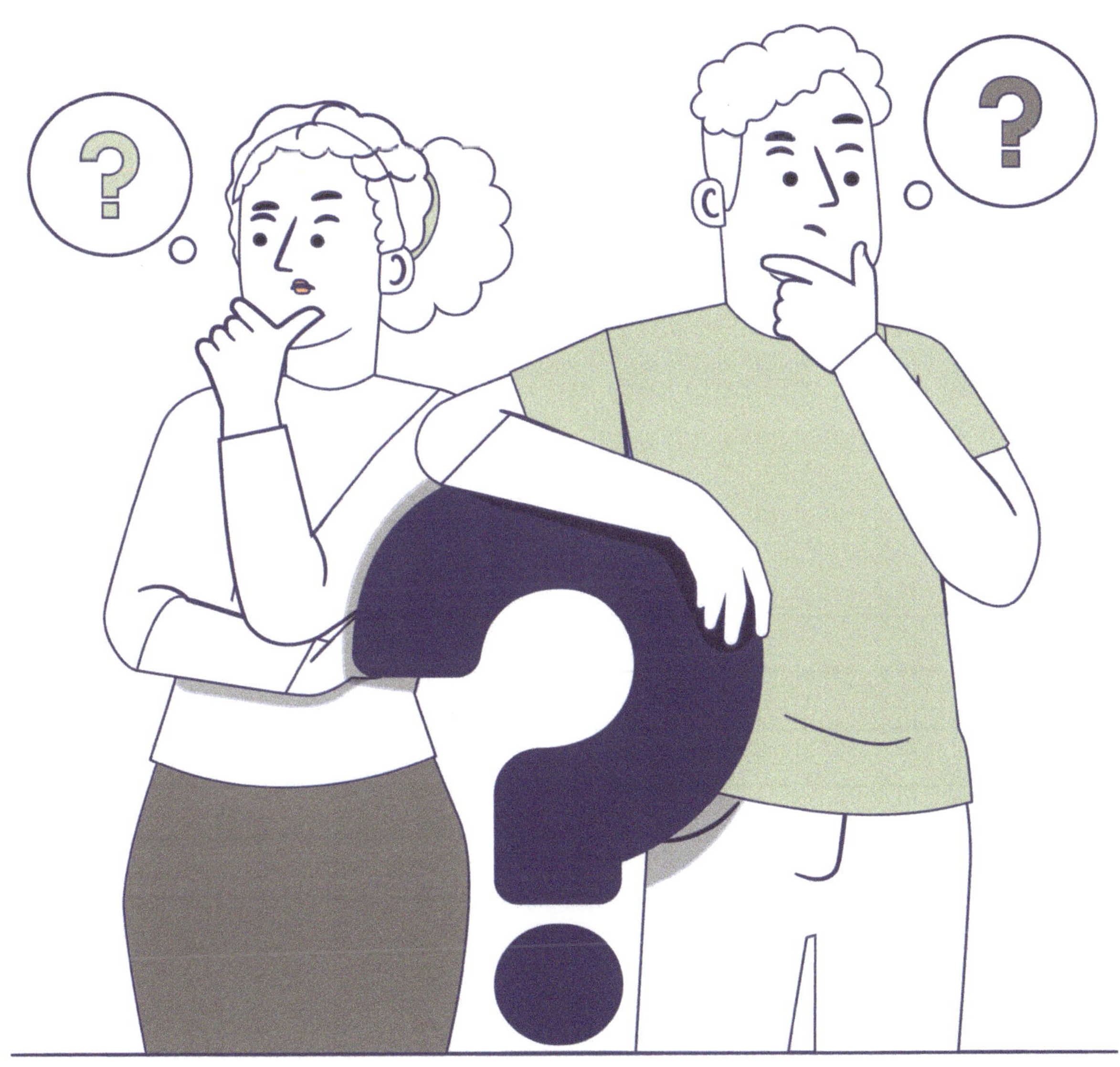

4 In (Height) X 6 In (Width)

Date:

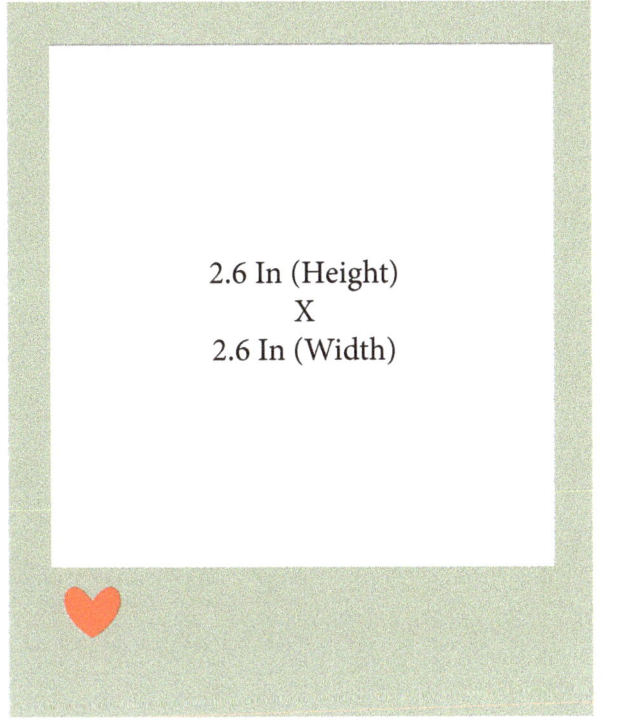

Date:

____
____
____
____
____
____

Date:

____
____
____
____
____
____

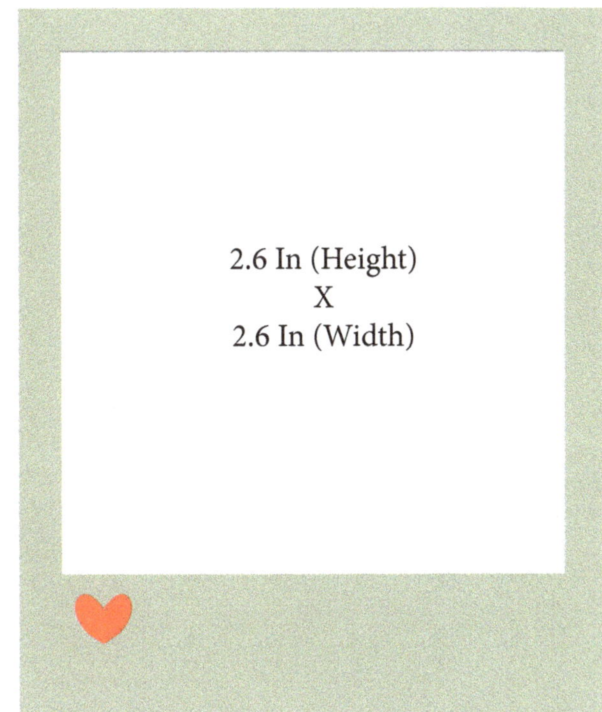

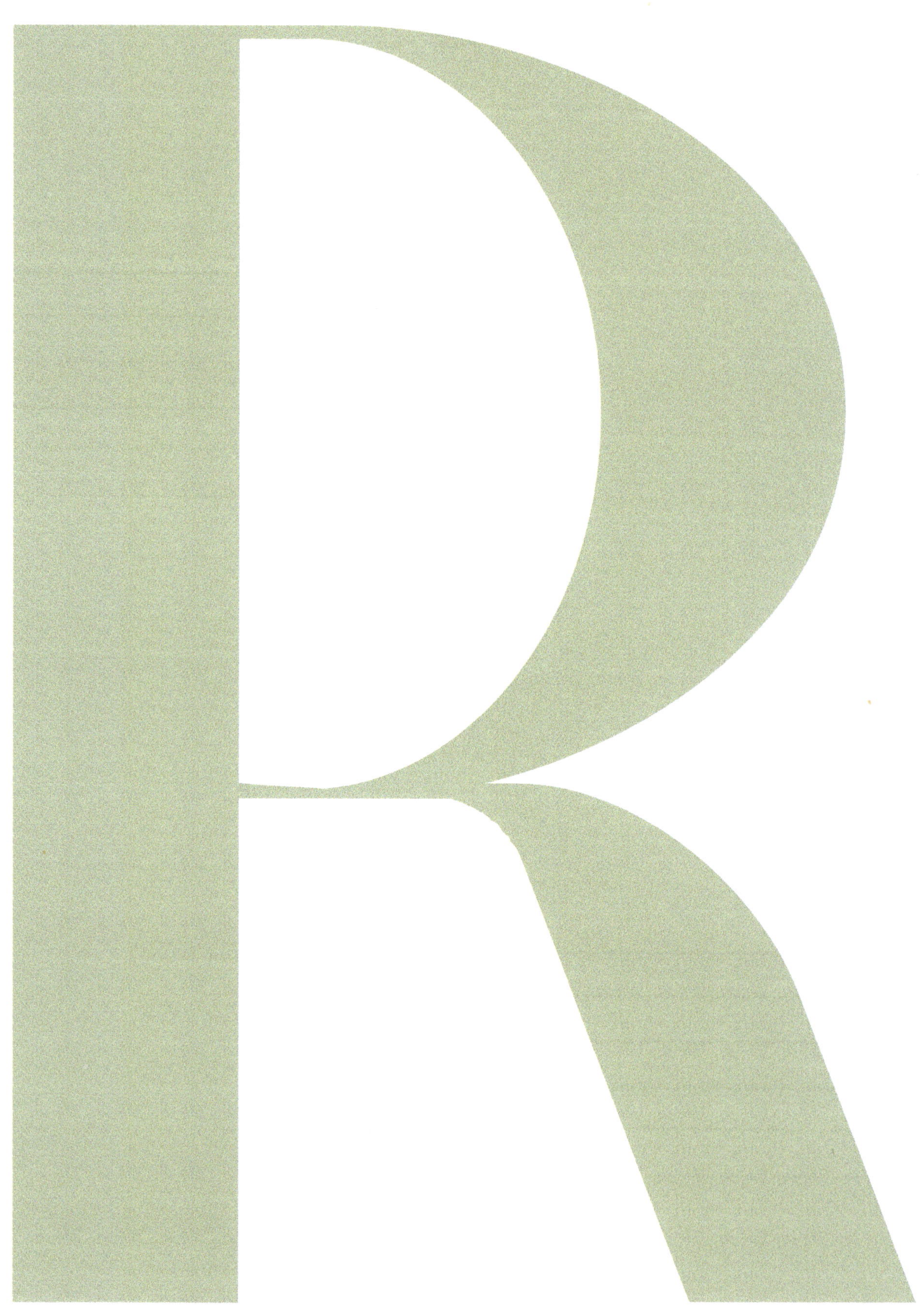

- Rodeo
- River rafting
- Roller skating
- Rock climbing
- Ring shopping
- Road trip
- Ring toss
- Roller coaster
- Riverboat date
- Rafting
- Racquetball
- Rent an exotic car
- Relaxation day
- Rent a boat
- Resort stay
- Rent a RV
- Rain forest visit
- Rooftop bar
- Rooftop pool

- Rooftop restaurant
- Restaurant of your choice
- Reptile exhibit
- Recipe exchange date
- Rescue a pet
- Random act of kindness
- Restore something old to new
- Remodel something
- Re-new your vous
- Re-make your favorite dinner dish
- Romantic movie marathon

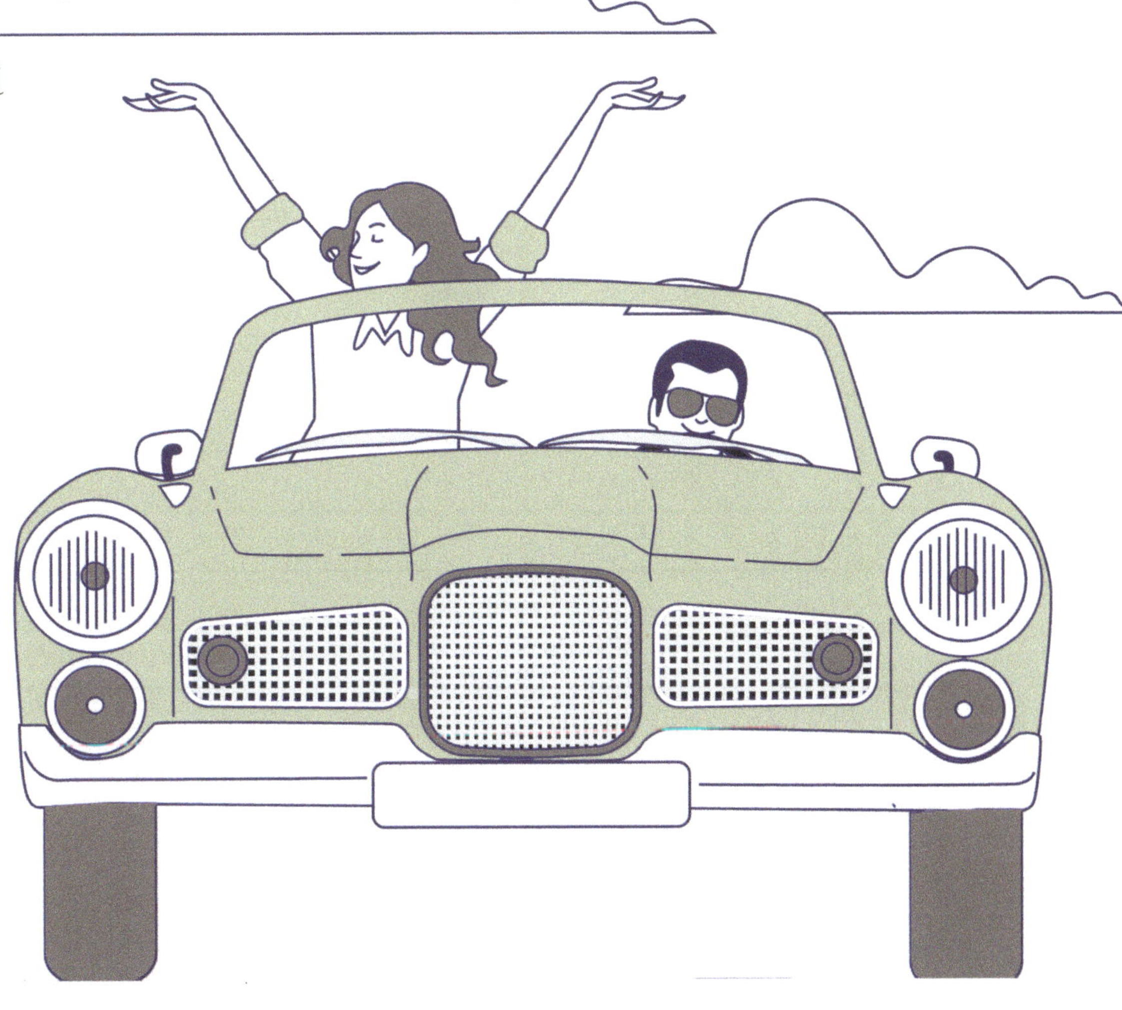

4 In (Height) X 6 In (Width)

Date:

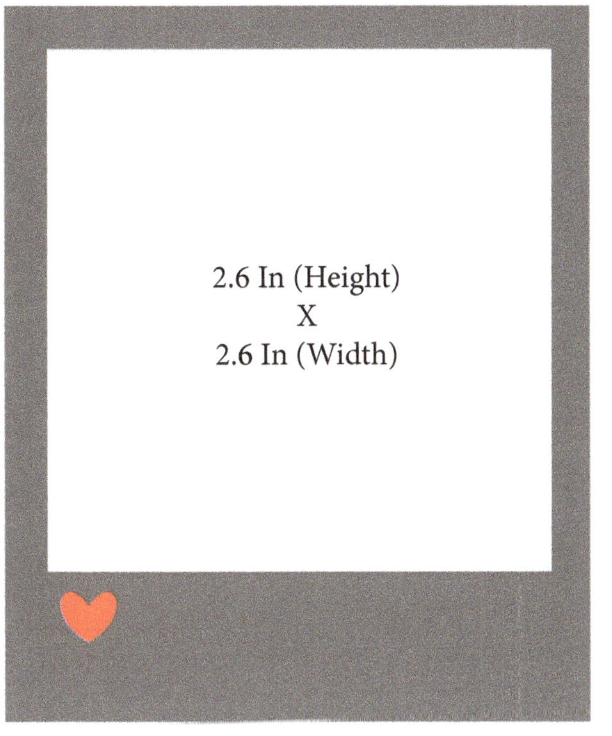

Date:

____

____

____

____

____

____

Date:

____

____

____

____

____

____

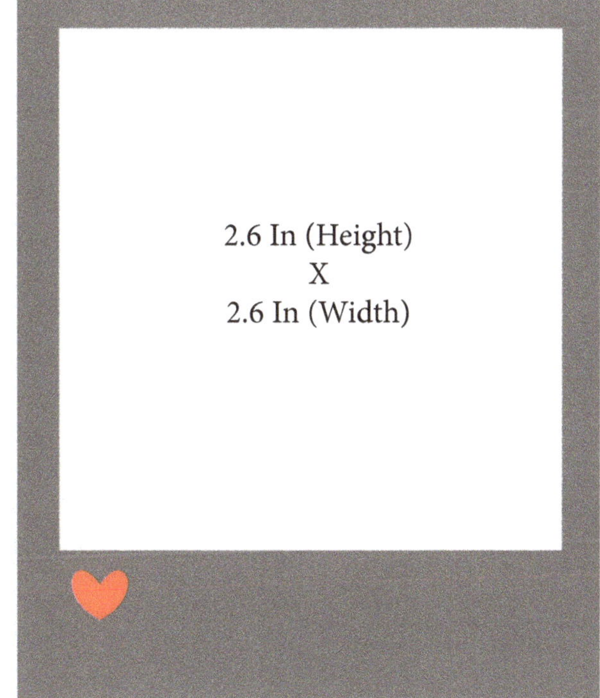

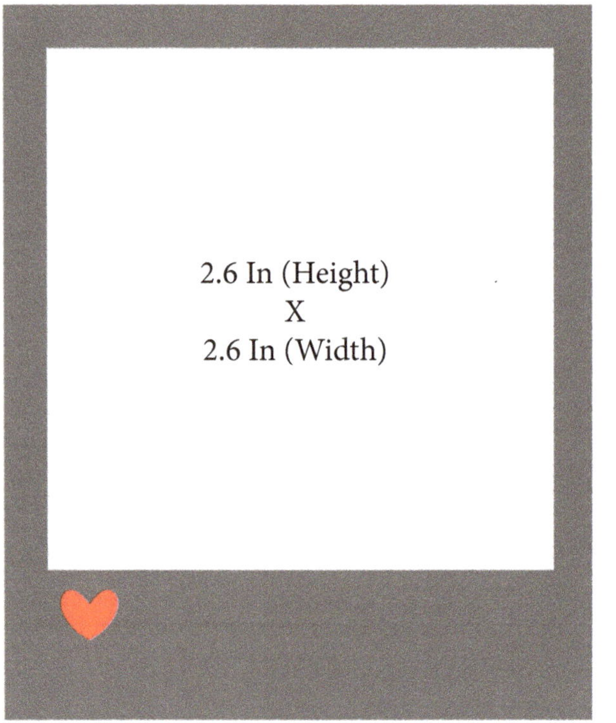

Date:

____

____

____

____

____

____

Date:

____

____

____

____

____

____

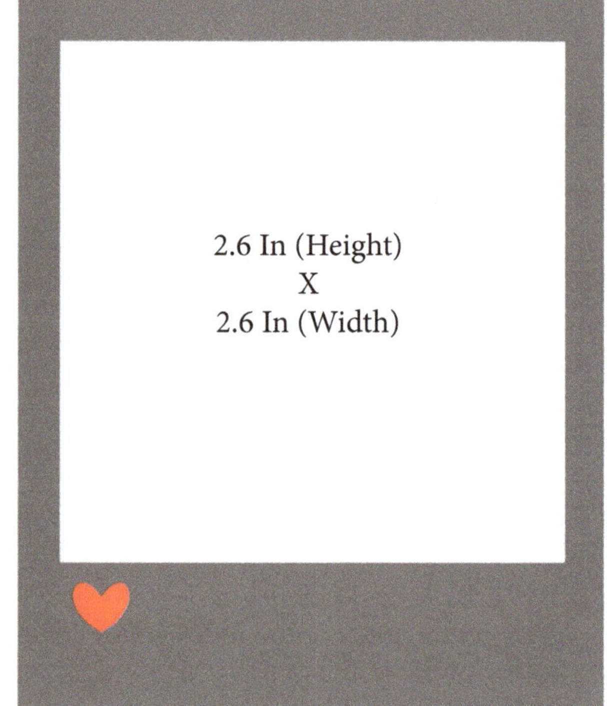

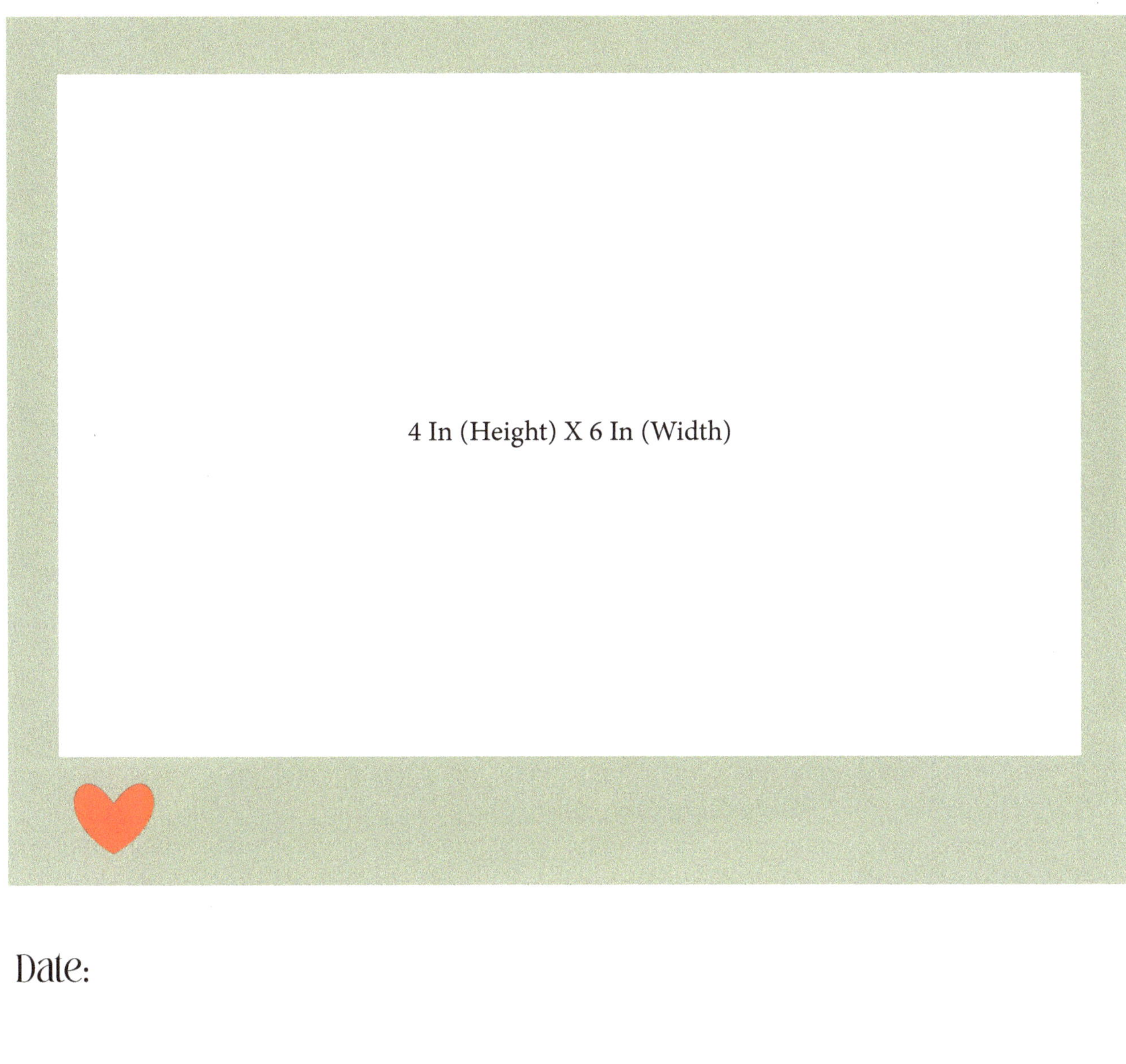

Date:

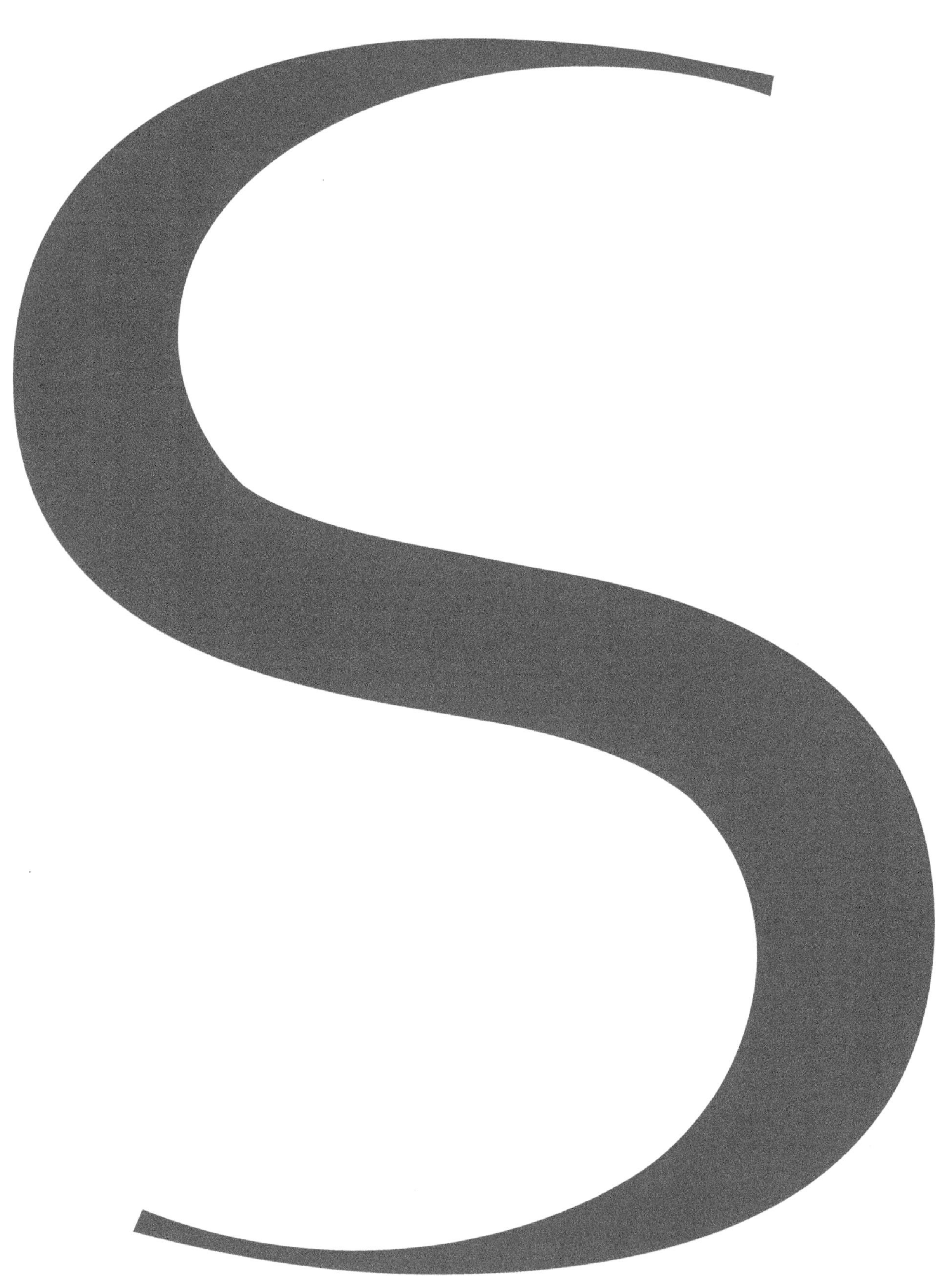

- Scavenger hunt
- Sewing classes
- Sushi making class
- Sightseeing
- Sunset movie
- Shooting range
- Skydiving
- Smore making
- SPIN class
- Street fair
- Slime making
- Shadow art
- Scrapbooking
- Soap making
- Scrabble date
- Spinning class
- Shopping spree
- Spa day
- Sports game
- Soccer game
- Six Flags
- Space museum
- Swimming date
- Skinny dipping
- Scuba diving
- Snorkeling
- Surfing
- Sailing
- Shuffleboard
- Sledding
- Snowboarding
- Skating
- Skiing
- Storm chasing
- Singing competition
- Star gazing
- Snuggling by a fire
- Scenery hike
- Seed planting
- Safari
- Sand castle making
- Sunrise
- Sunset
- Something you have been wanting to do for a long time

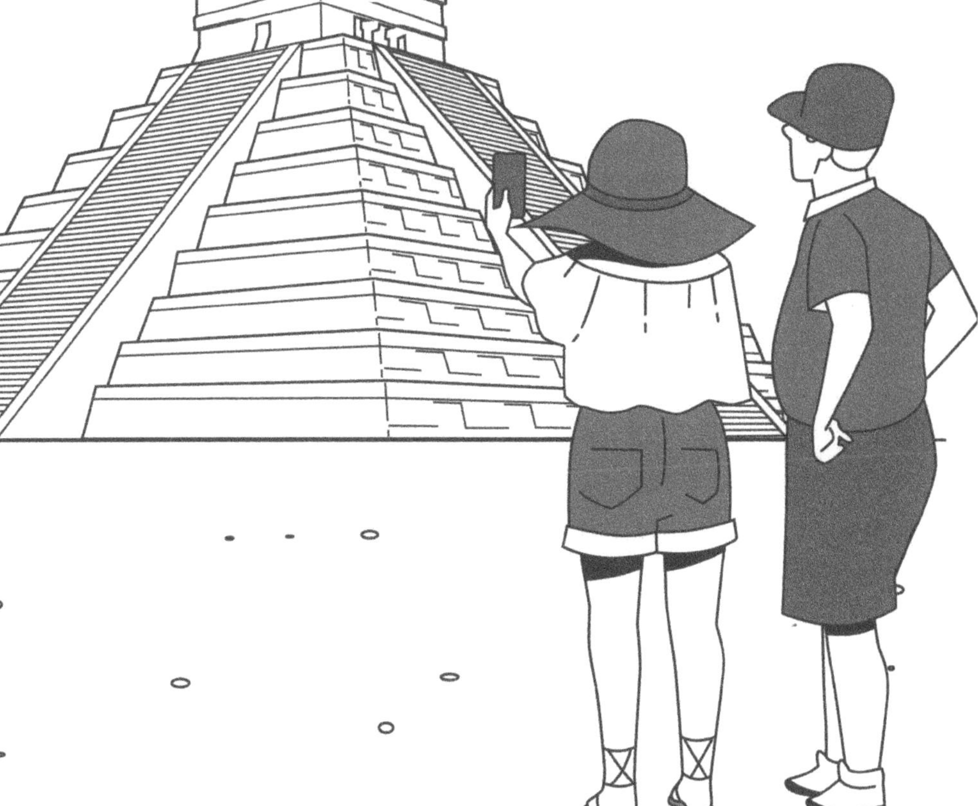

4 In (Height) X 6 In (Width)

Date:

____

____

____

____

____

____

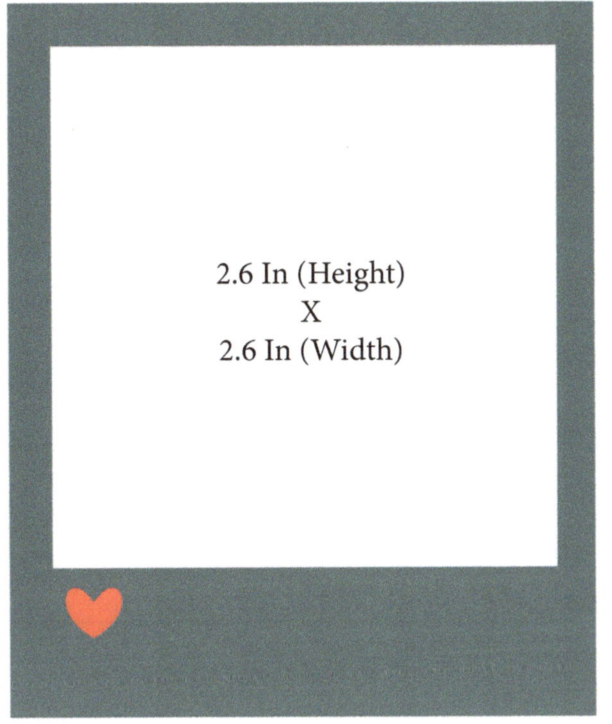

Date:

____

____

____

____

____

____

Date:

____

____

____

____

____

____

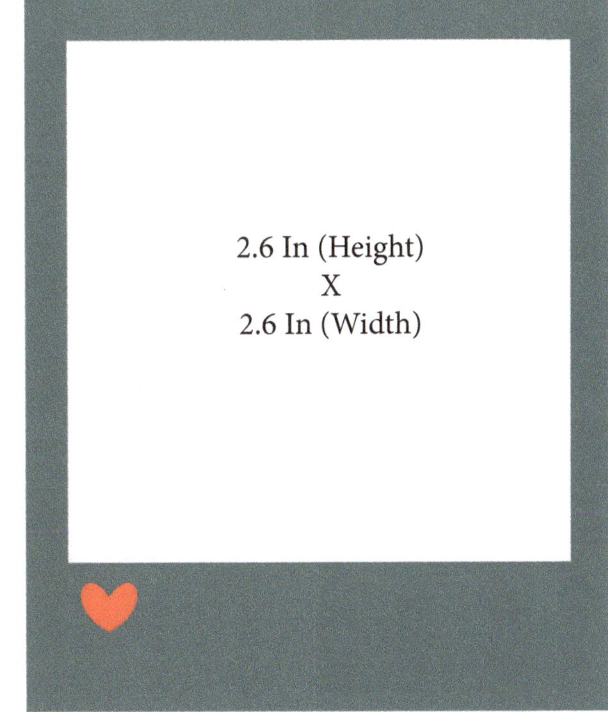

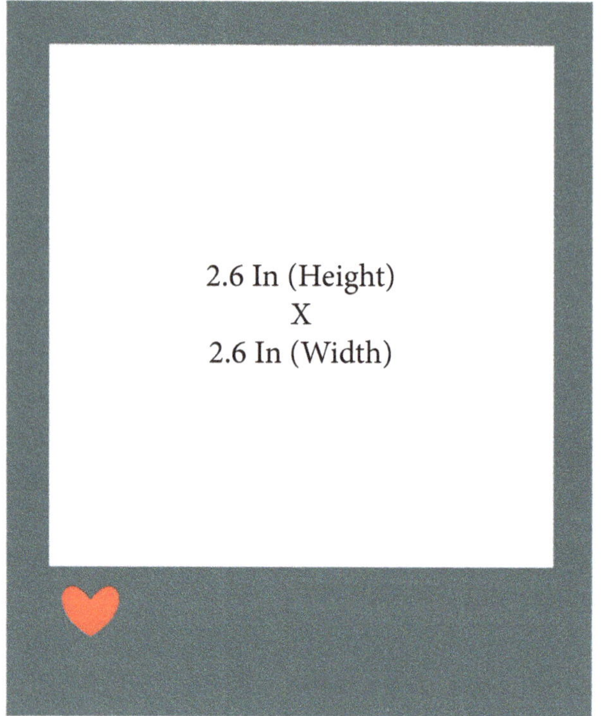

Date:

____
____
____
____
____
____

Date:

____
____
____
____
____
____

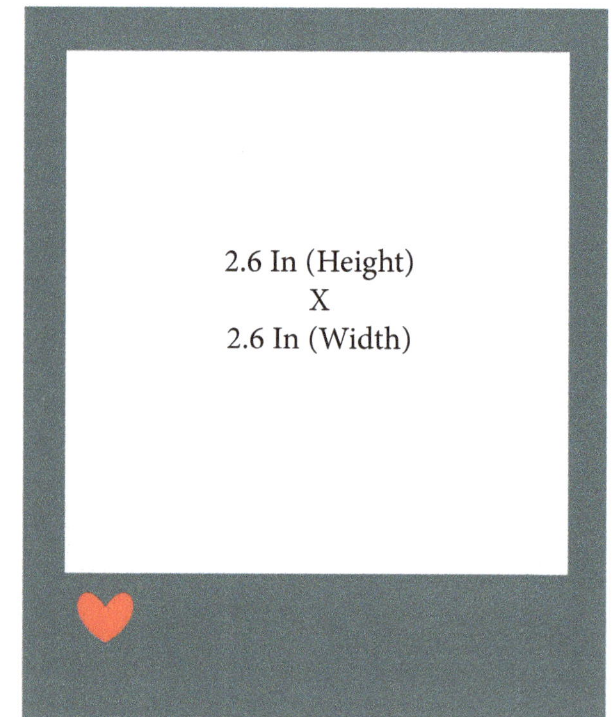

4 In (Height) X 6 In (Width)

Date:
____
____
____
____
____
____

- Trivia night
- Tennis date
- Taco night
- Thrift store shopping
- Tour something new
- Travel to a new destination
- Tree climbing
- Treasure hunt
- Tailgate at a scenic place
- TopGolf date
- Trampoline park
- Theme park
- Tubing (snow/water)
- Theater

- Test drive a new car
- Train ride to somewhere new
- Tap dancing class
- Trapeze lesson
- Tickets to a show/game
- Talk show
- Taste testing
- Tattoo date
- Tie Dye something
- Technology free date
- Themed date
- Treat yourself to something new/ fun

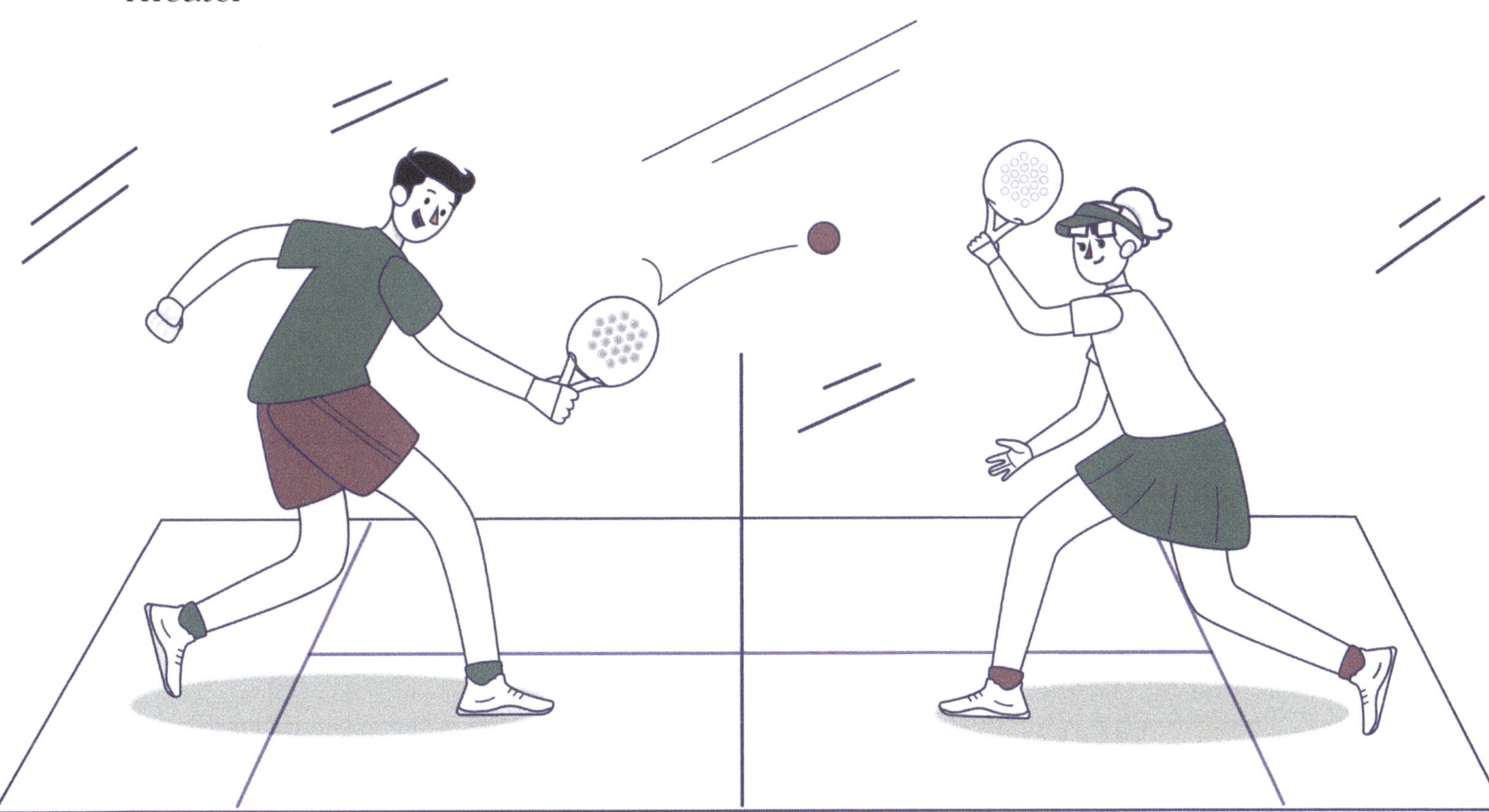

4 In (Height) X 6 In (Width)

Date:
____
____
____
____
____
____

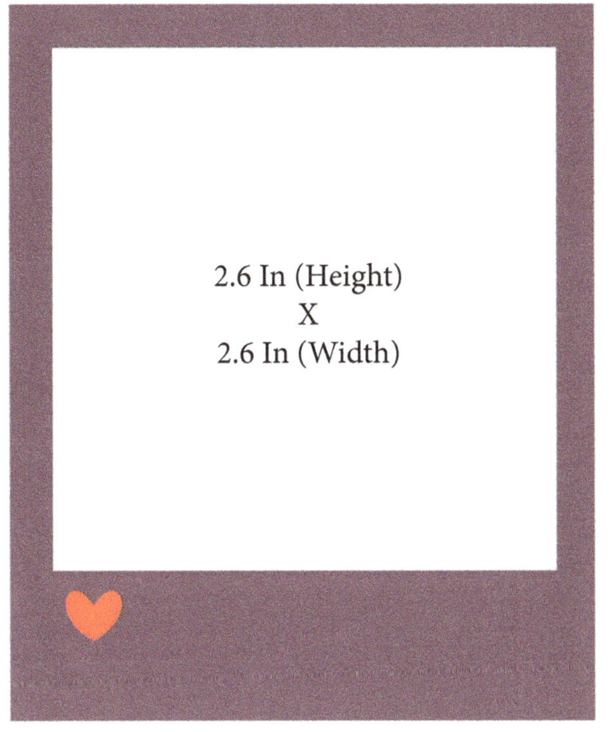

Date:

Date:

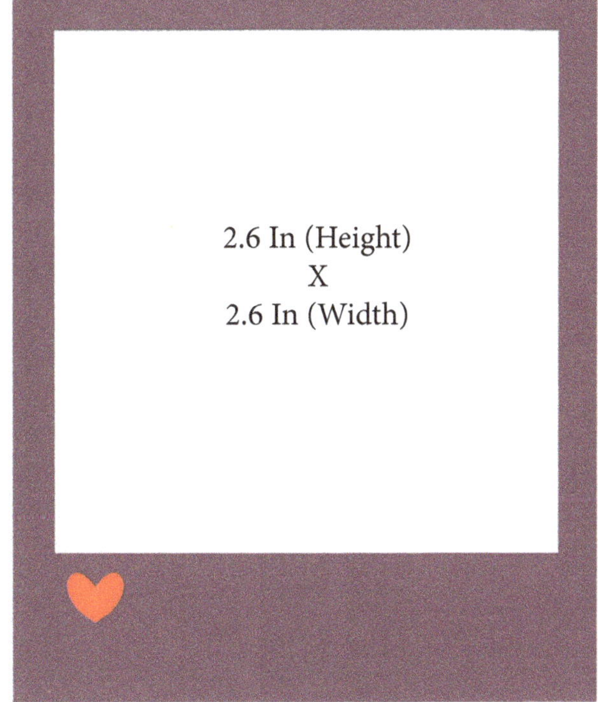

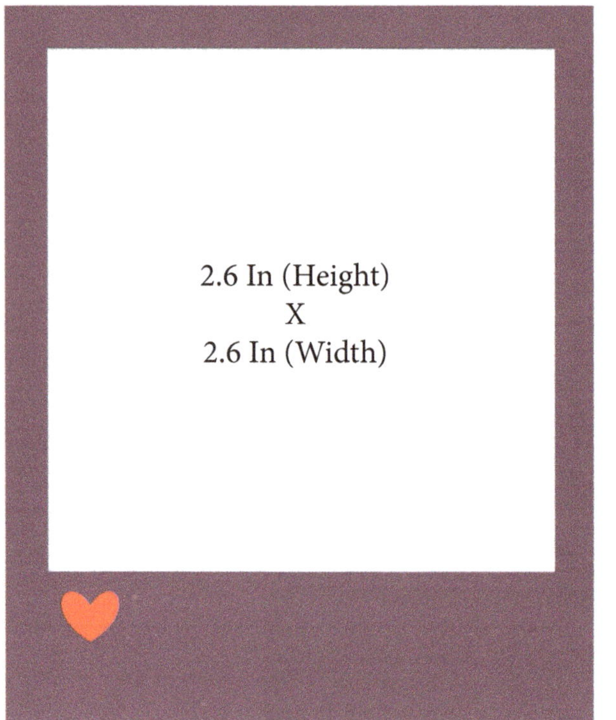

Date:

____

____

____

____

____

____

Date:

____

____

____

____

____

____

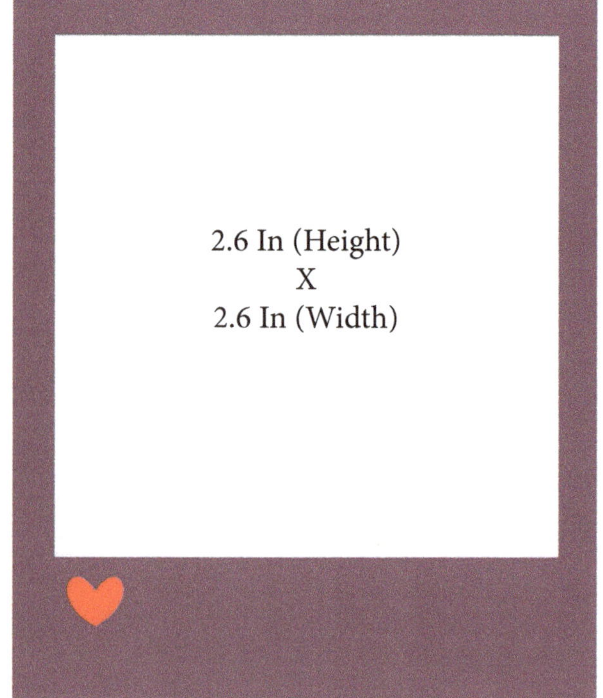

4 In (Height) X 6 In (Width)

Date:

- Upscale dinner
- Ultimate frisbee
- Ugly sweater shopping
- Universal studios day trip
- Underwater cave exploring
- Underwater diving
- Underwater swimming
- University baseball game
- Up-lighting movie
- Unplugged evening
- Under the sea date (restaurant)

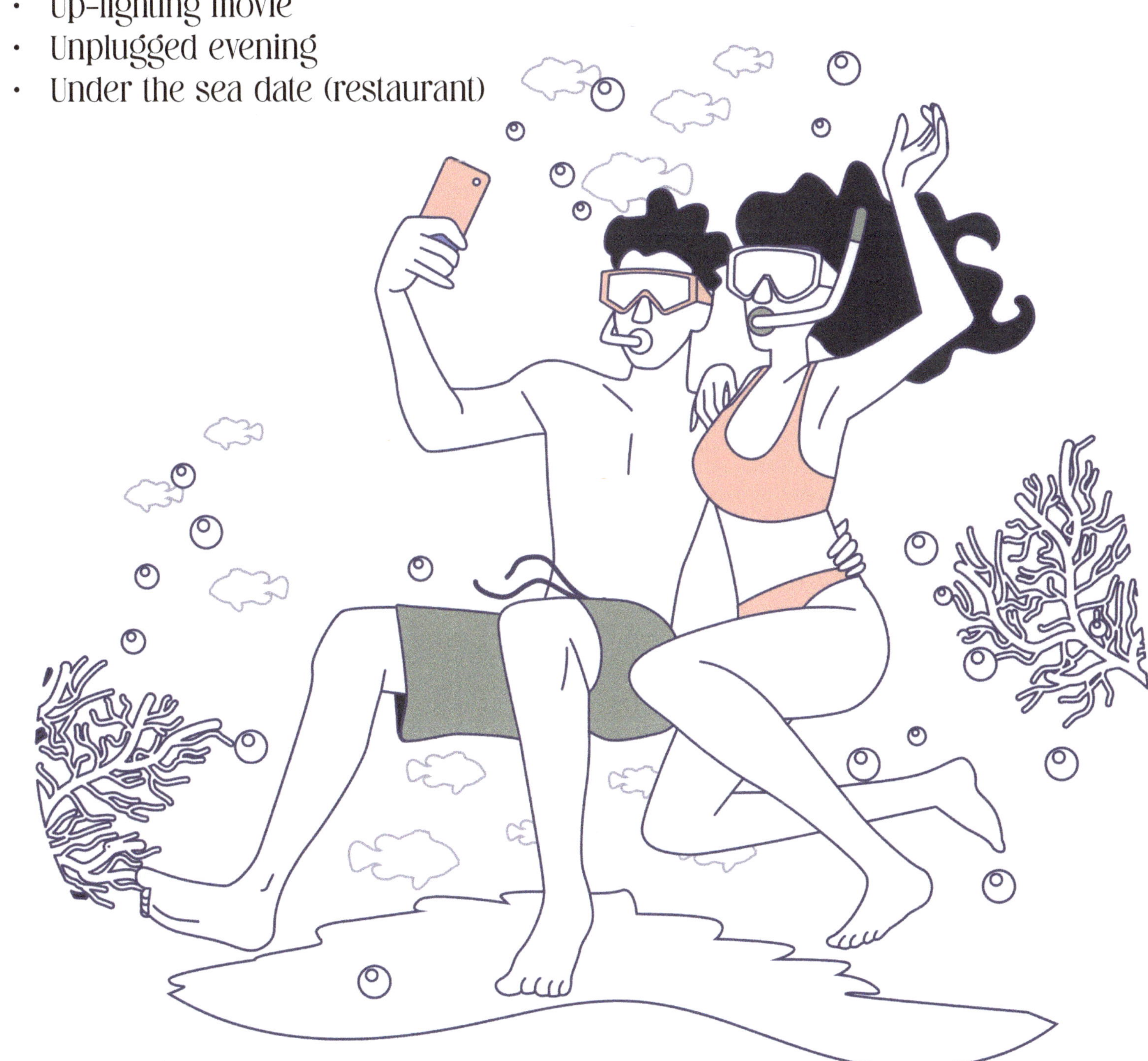

4 In (Height) X 6 In (Width)

Date:

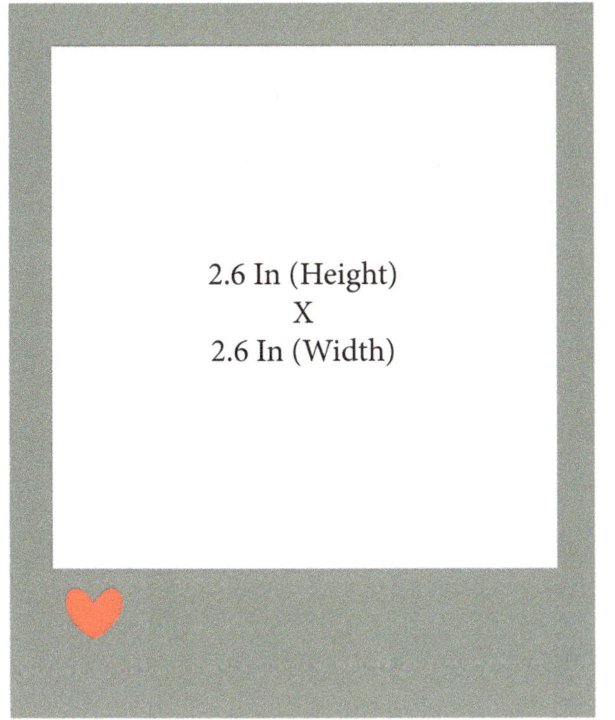

Date:

____

____

____

____

____

____

Date:

____

____

____

____

____

____

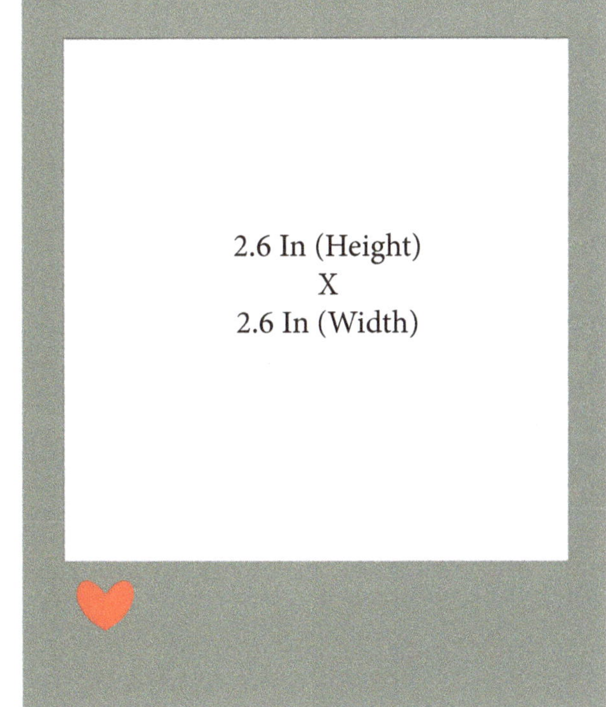

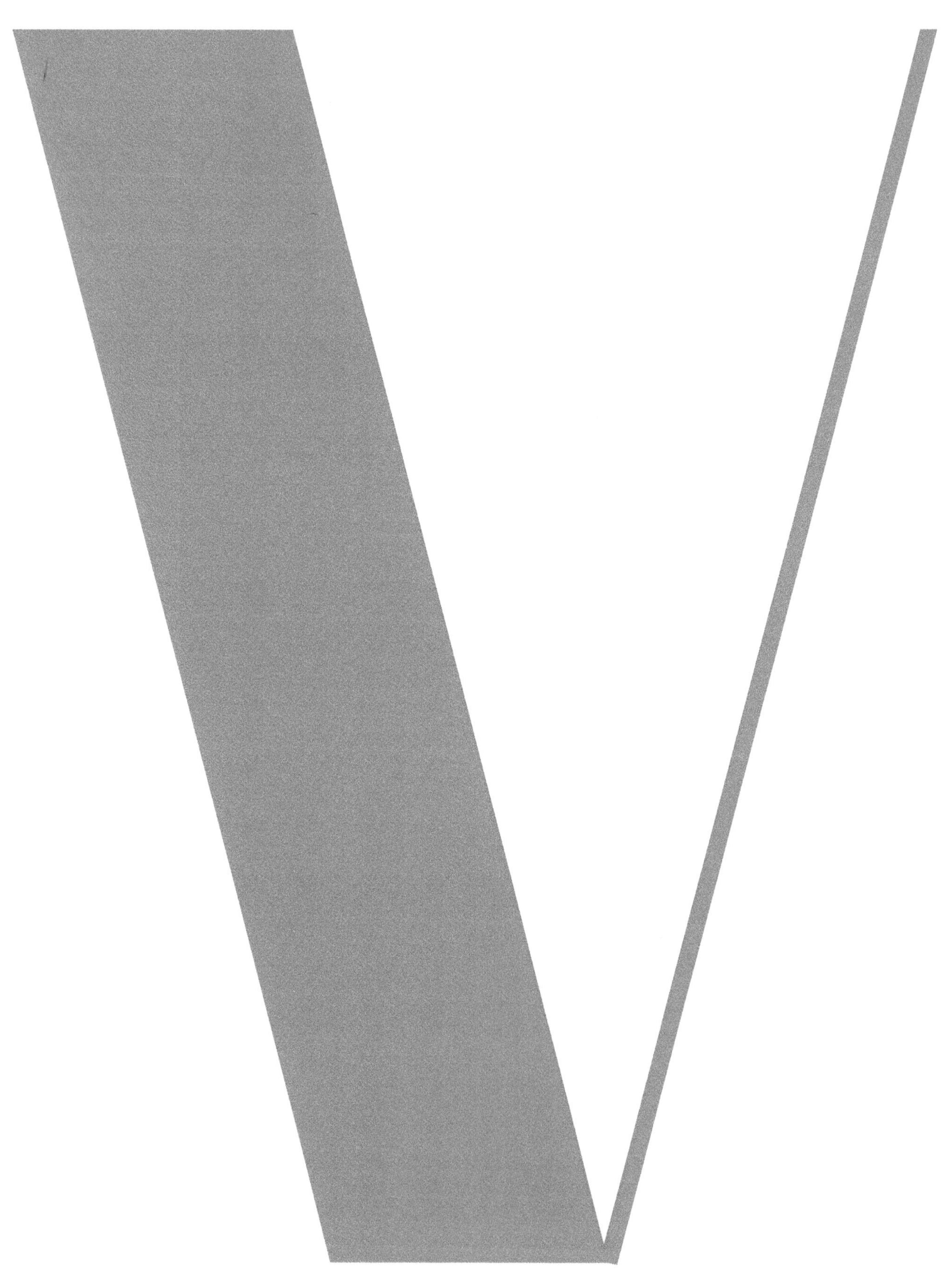

- Virtual wine tastings
- Virtual reality games
- Volleyball
- Video game competition
- Videography
- Vacation to somewhere new
- Vase making/decorating
- Valentine's date
- Volunteer
- Visit friends for a double date
- Vegetable picking
- Varsity football game
- Volcano tour

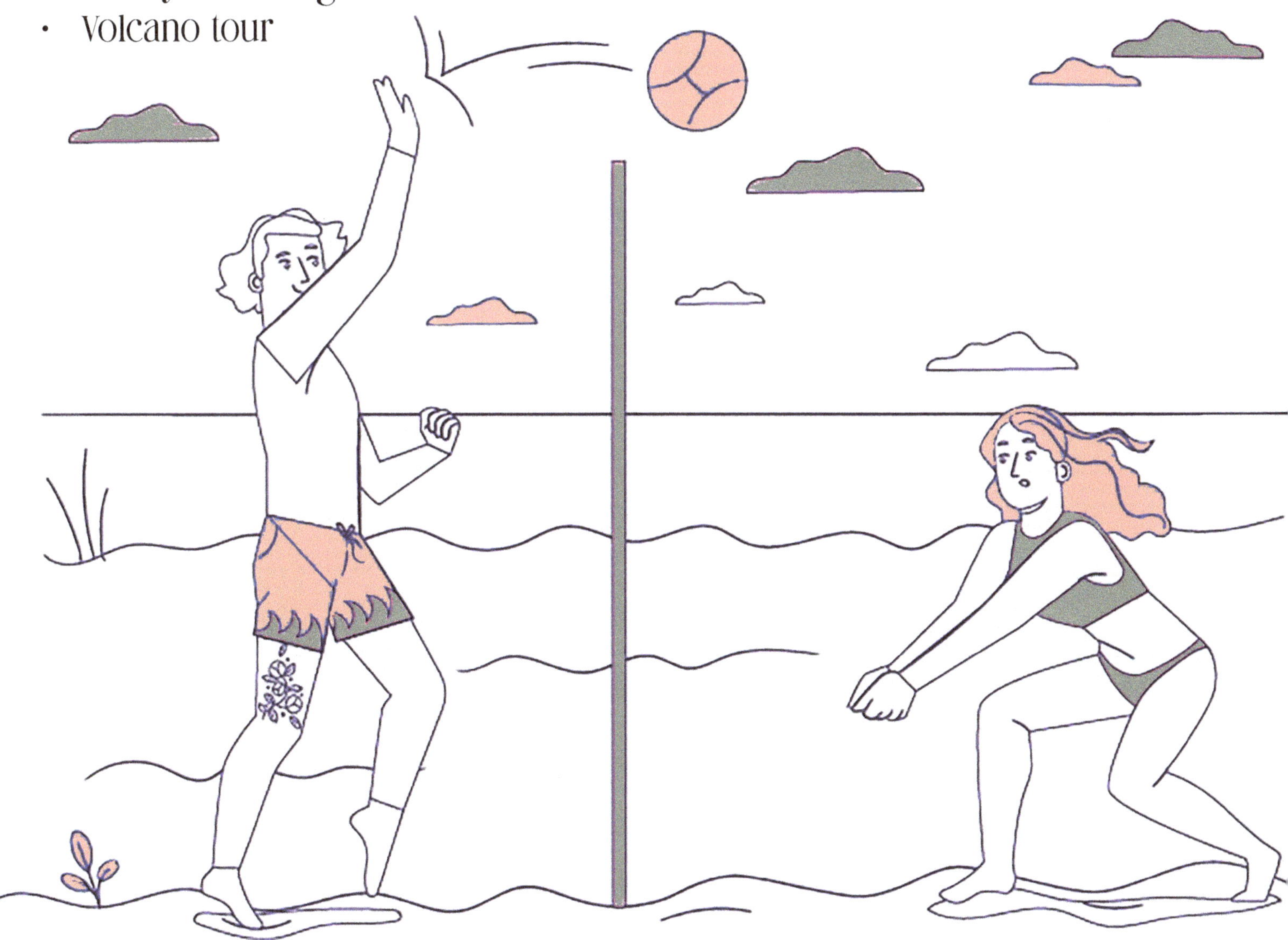

4 In (Height) X 6 In (Width)

Date:

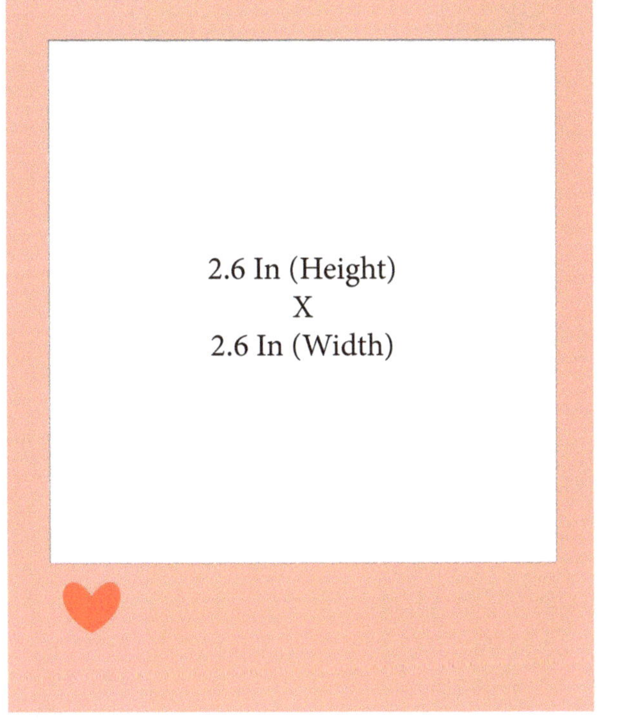

Date:

____

____

____

____

____

____

Date:

____

____

____

____

____

____

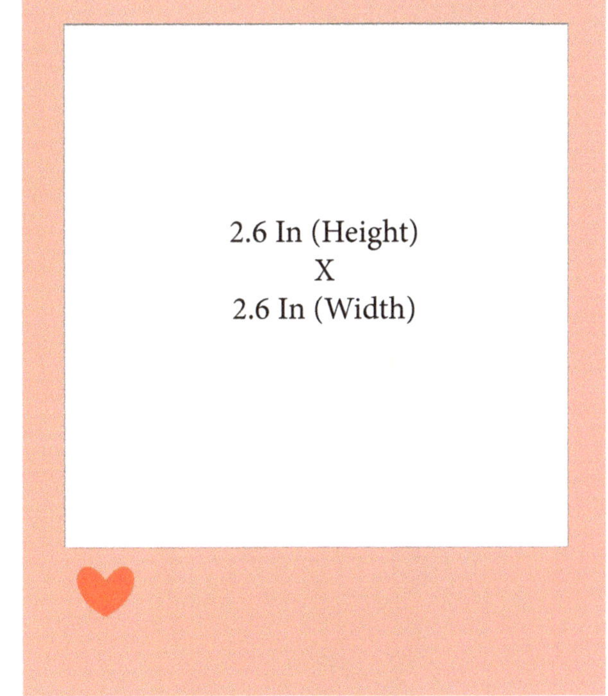

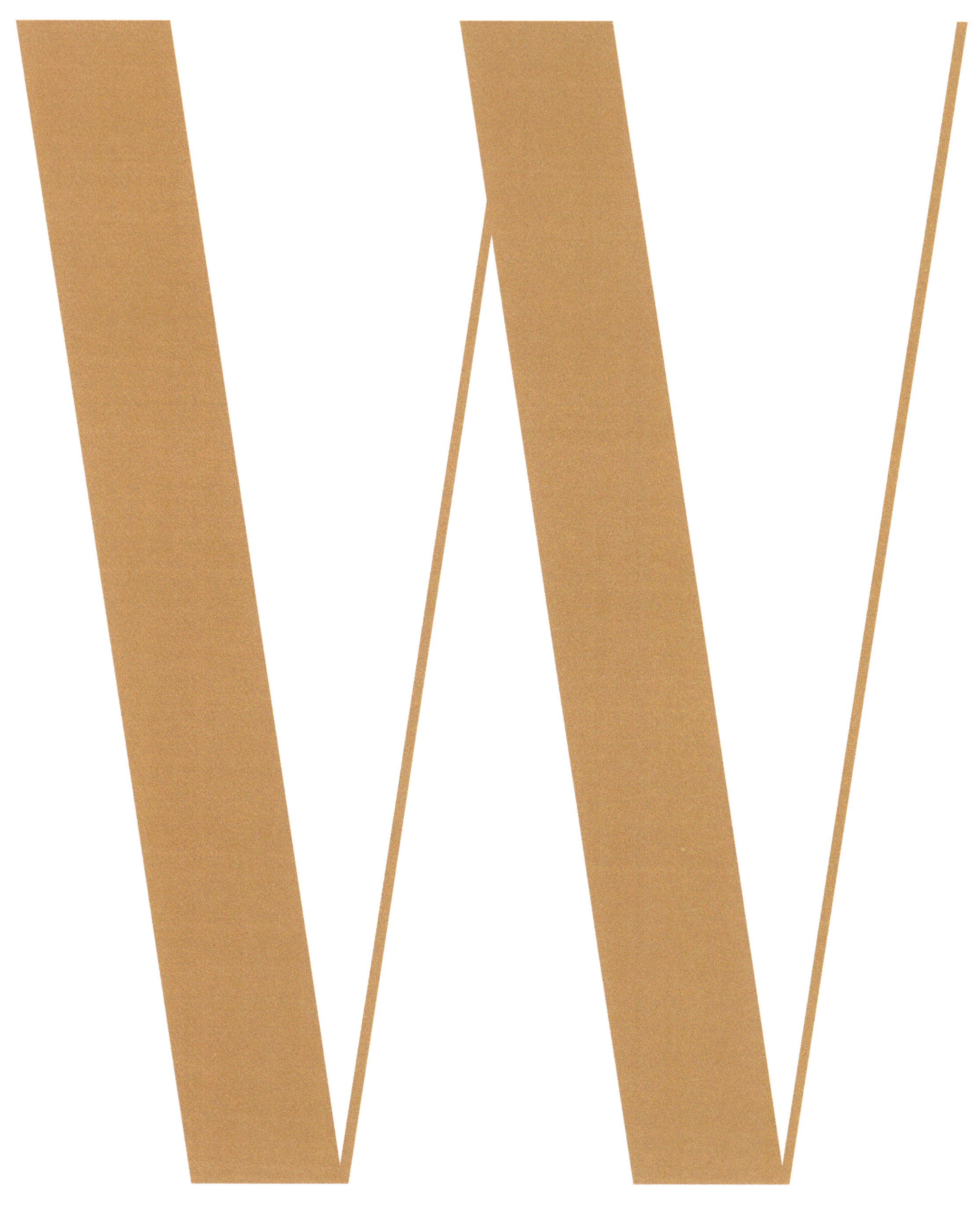

- Woodworking classes
- Whale watching
- Waterfall finding
- White water rafting
- Winery tour
- Wine tastings
- Winery bar crawl
- Workout session
- Wax museum
- Wax making
- Wildlife adventure
- Water park
- Waterfall exploration
- Wind sailing
- Wind surfing
- Water skiing
- Wakeboarding
- Wiffle ball
- Wrestling
- Winter themed date
- Wagon ride
- Weight lifting
- Weekend getaway
- Window shopping
- Wander around & see w here you end up
- Western themed date
- Water color painting

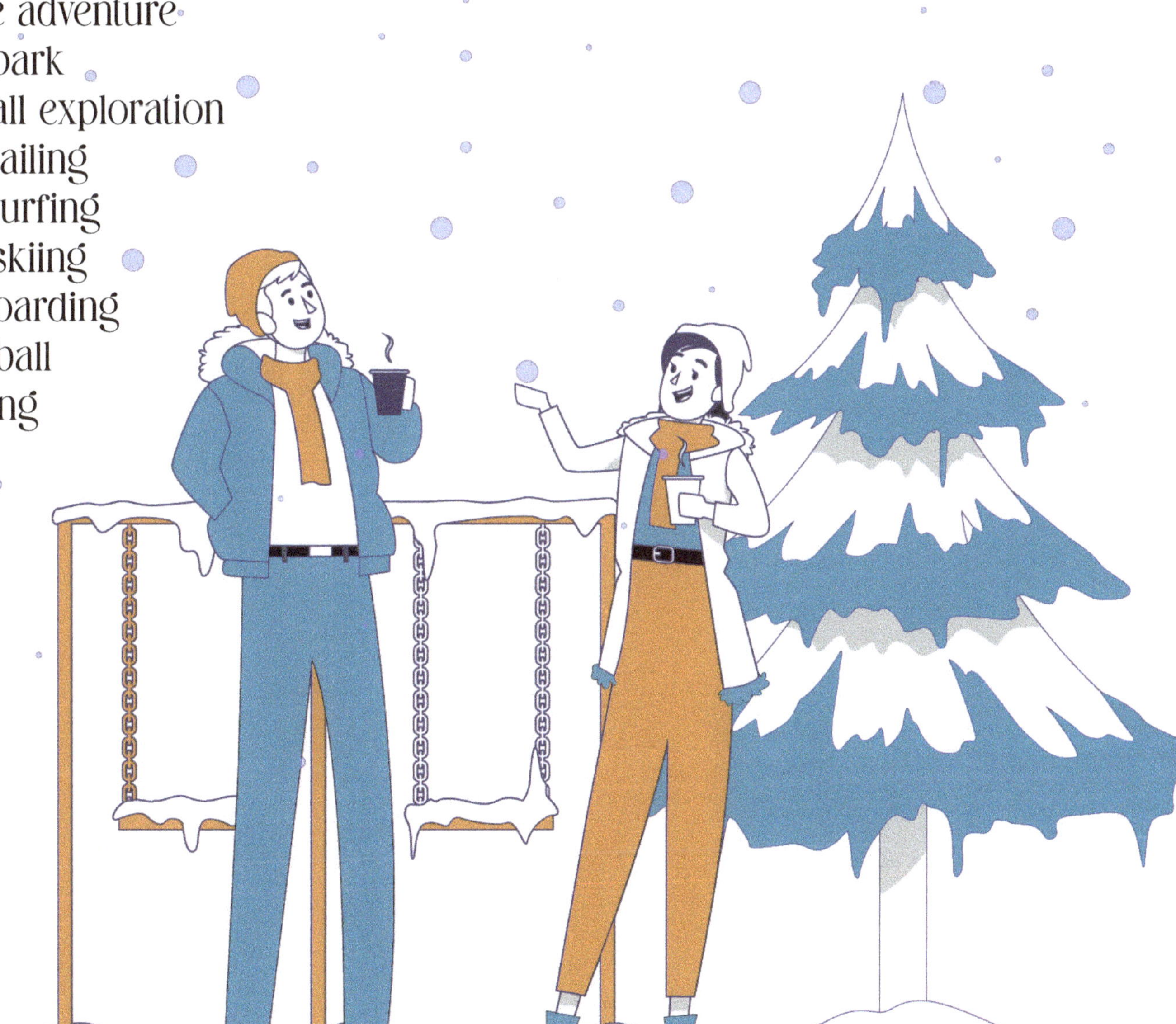

4 In (Height) X 6 In (Width)

Date:

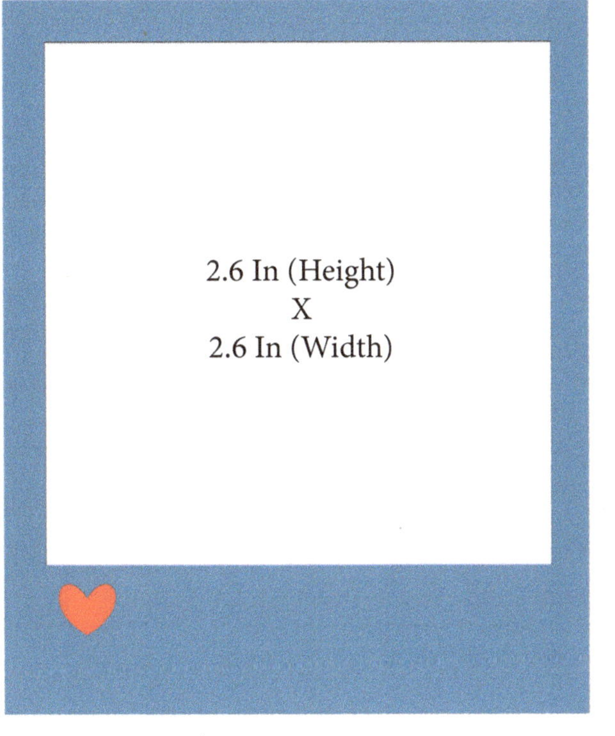

Date:

____
____
____
____
____
____

Date:

____
____
____
____
____
____

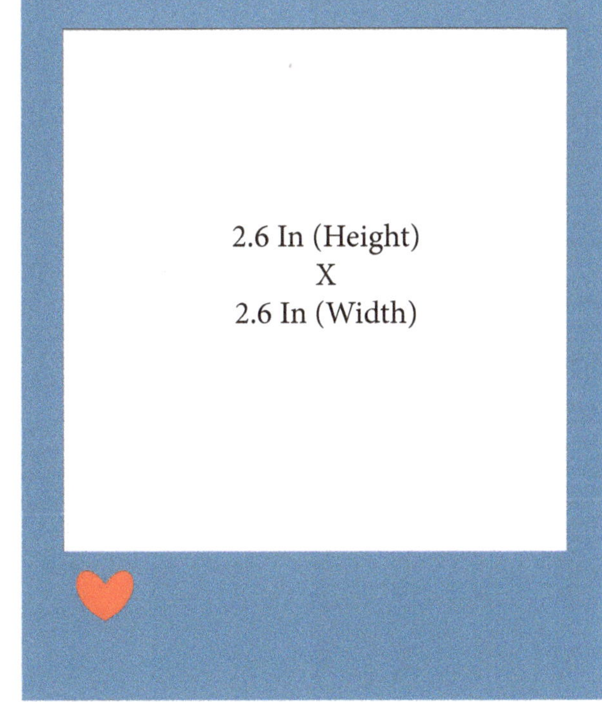

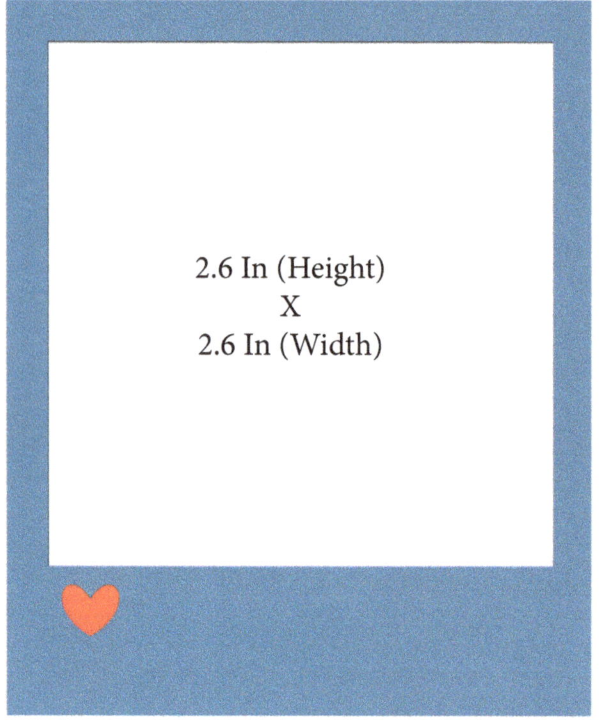

Date:

____

____

____

____

____

____

Date:

____

____

____

____

____

____

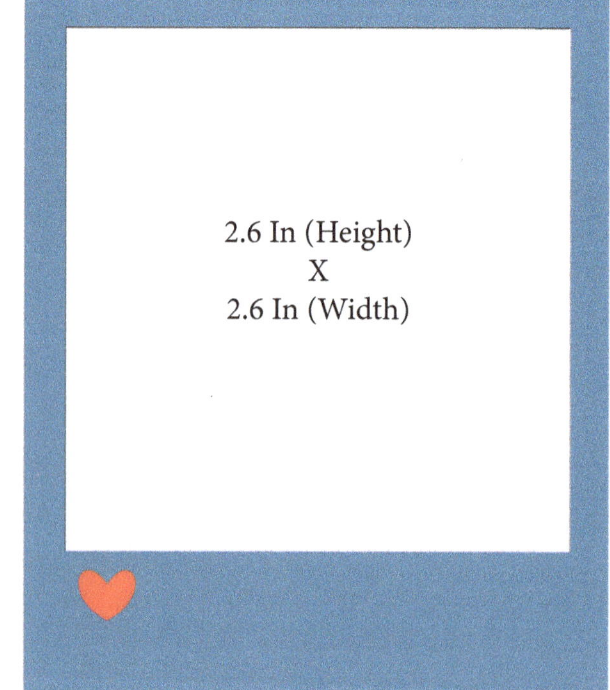

4 In (Height) X 6 In (Width)

Date:
____
____
____
____
____
____

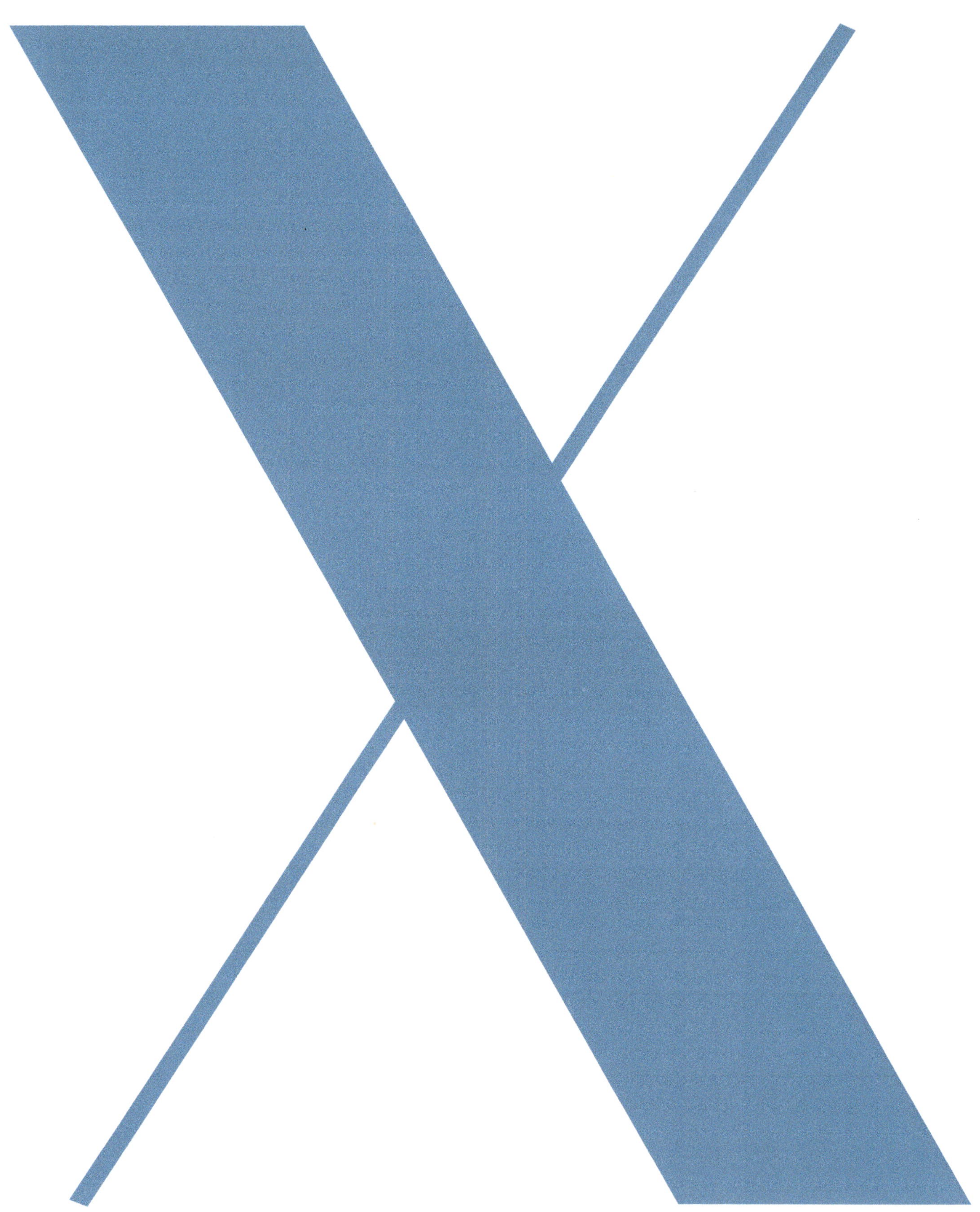

- Xbox tournament
- X-games
- X marks the spot – scavenger hunt
- X-mas themed date
- X & O's game (Tic-Tac-Toe)
- X-Men film marathon

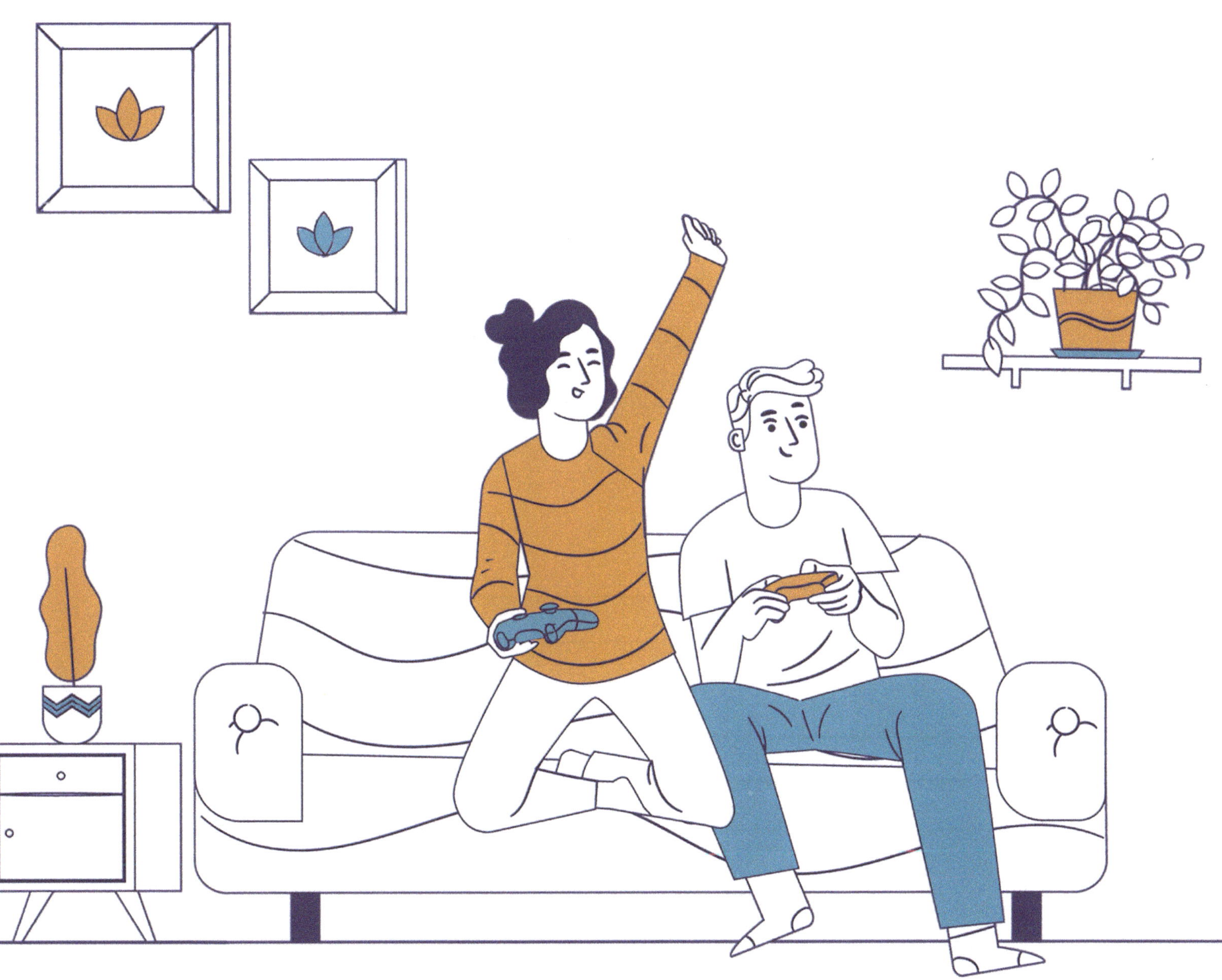

4 In (Height) X 6 In (Width)

Date:

2.6 In (Height)
X
2.6 In (Width)

Date:

Date:

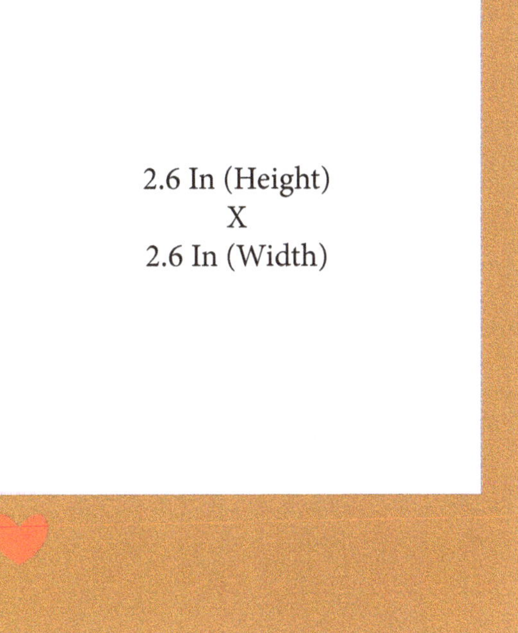

2.6 In (Height)
X
2.6 In (Width)

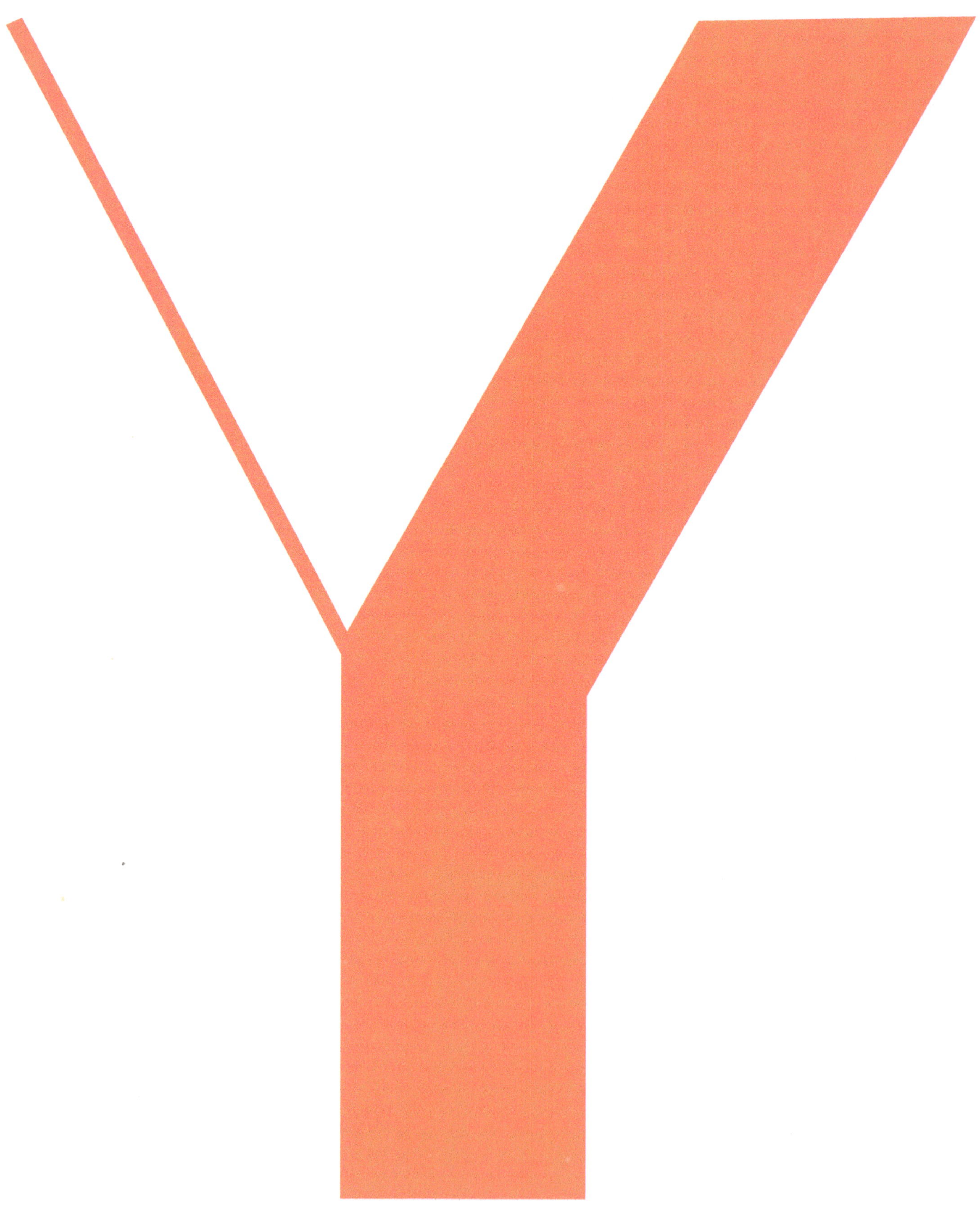

- Yoga
- Yellowstone binge night
- Yard sale date
- Yes day
- Yacht day
- Yellow themed date
- YouTube binge
- Yahtzee game
- Yogurt shop
- Yard games

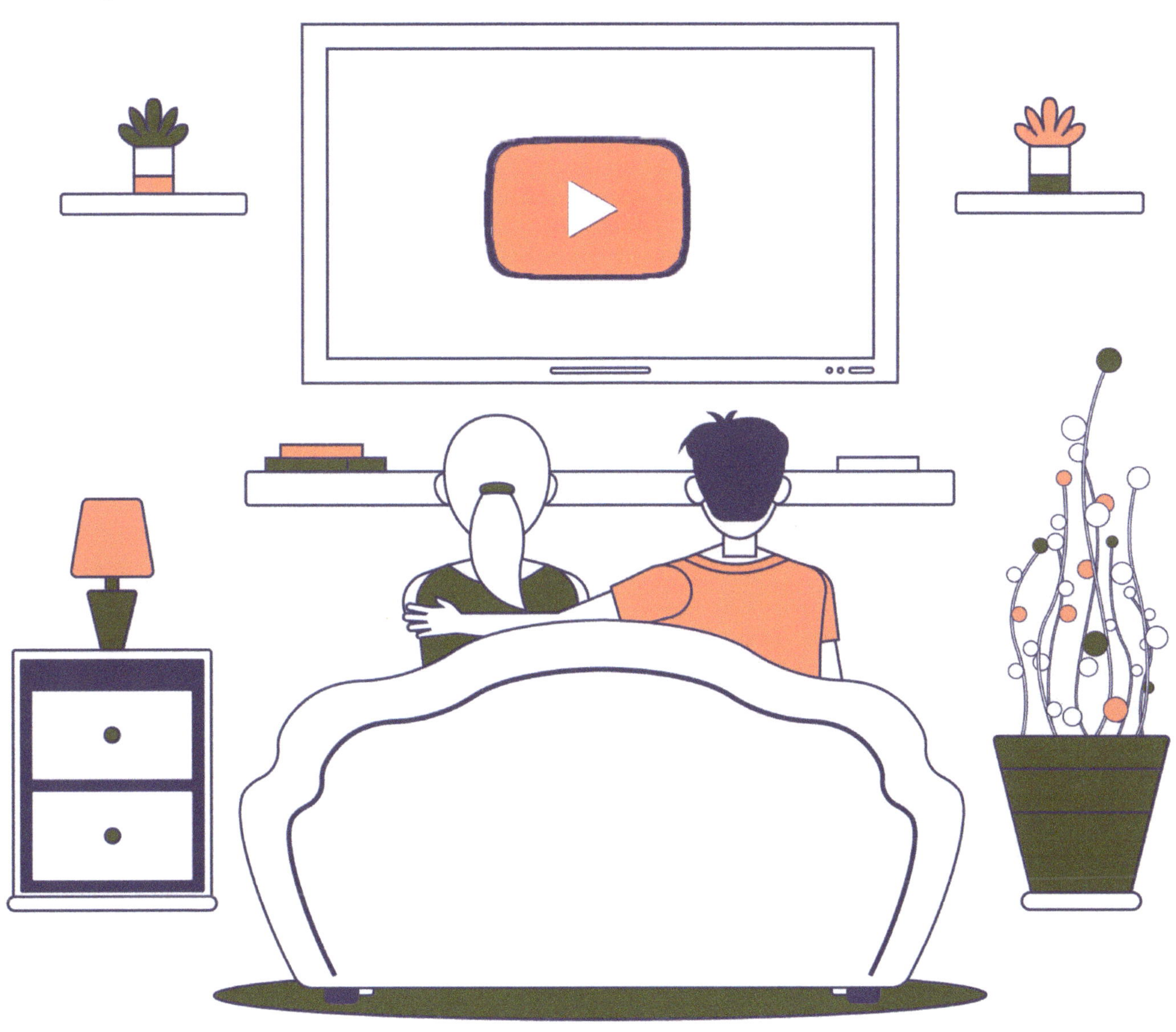

4 In (Height) X 6 In (Width)

Date:

____

____

____

____

____

____

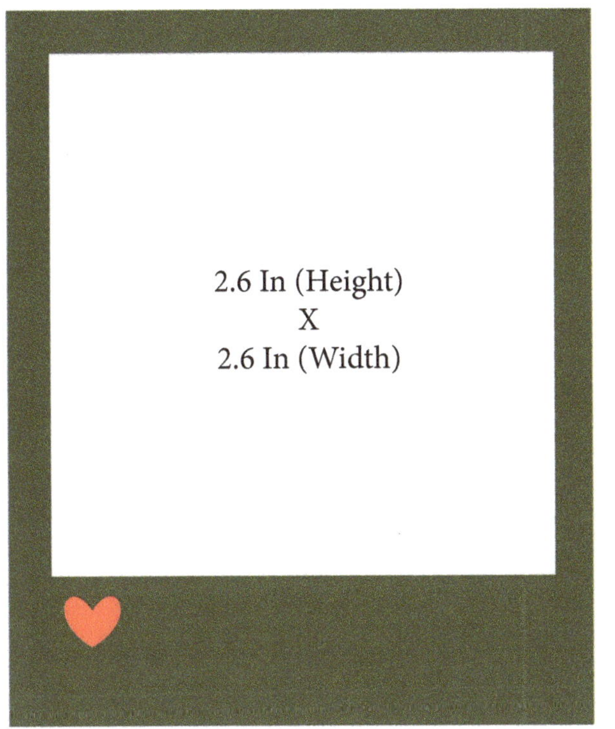
2.6 In (Height)
X
2.6 In (Width)

Date:

Date:

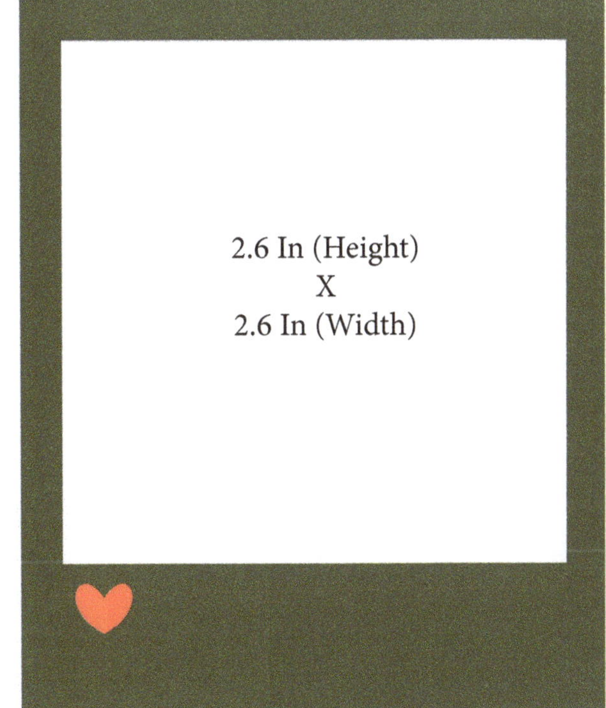
2.6 In (Height)
X
2.6 In (Width)

- Zoo day
- Ziplining
- Zero gravity experience
- Zumba class
- Zoom date

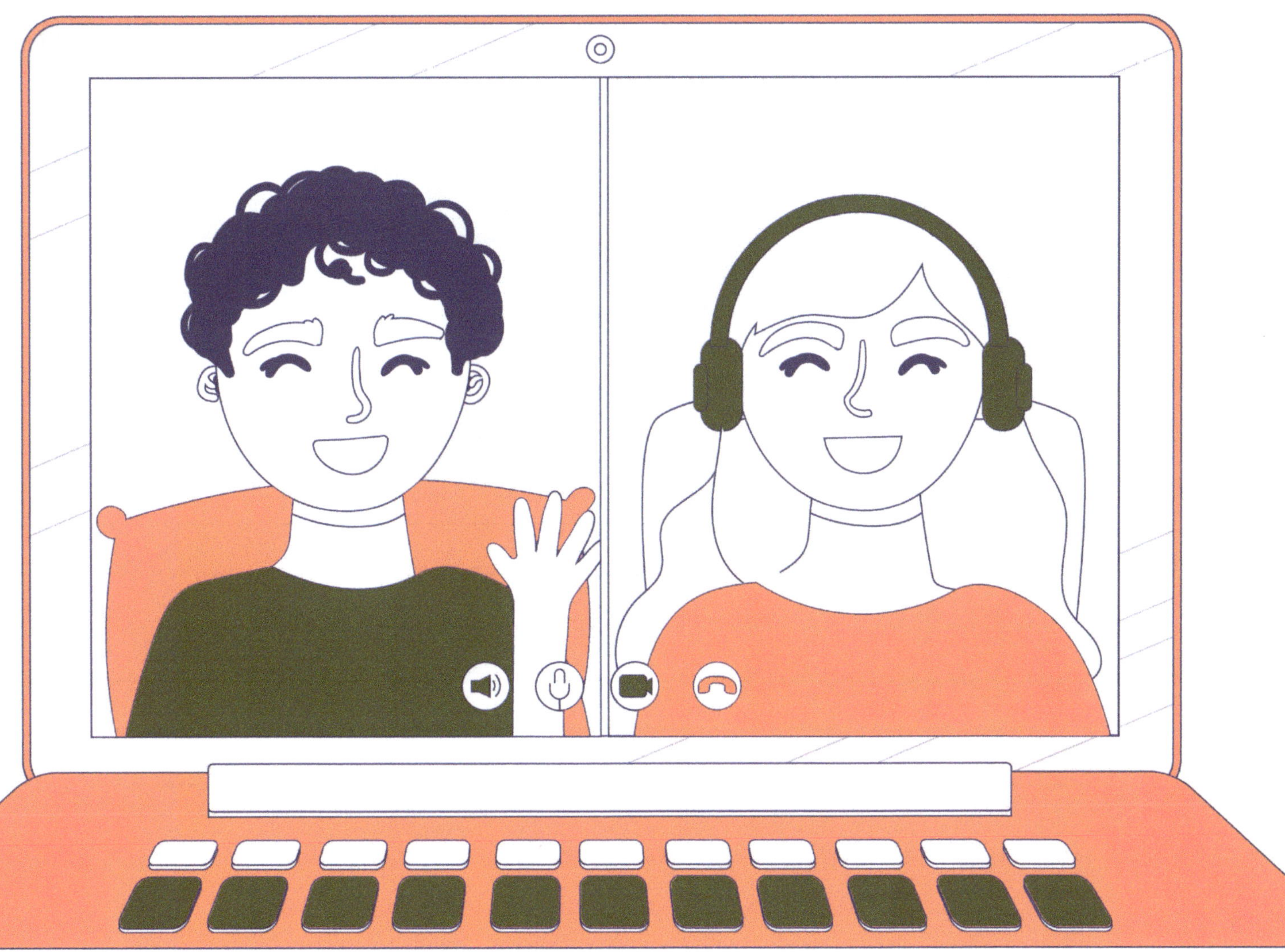

4 In (Height) X 6 In (Width)

Date:

2.6 In (Height)
X
2.6 In (Width)

Date:

____

____

____

____

____

____

Date:

____

____

____

____

____

____

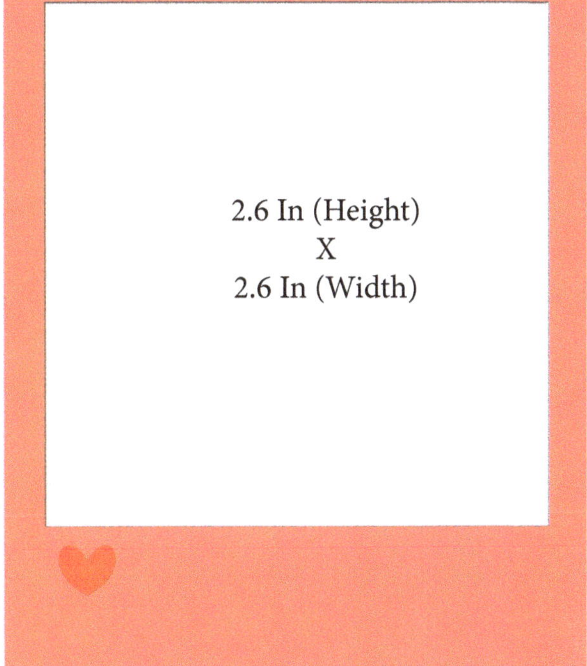